S0-CFC-507

Preface

Years ago I had the good fortune to come across a book that shattered my way of looking at the world. That book was *Eros and Civilization* by Herbert Marcuse. Like others of my generation, I came away from Marcuse haunted by the terrible bleakness of social life. Why, Marcuse made me wonder, does all the progress in our moral and social lives do so little to end human misery and destructiveness? Why, instead of liberating us to enjoy life, does so much of morality and conscience teach us to repress our most natural passions? Whence comes this "fateful antagonism" of culture to human nature, as if who we are naturally is irredeemably sinful and evil? To read *Eros and Civilization* was to yearn for a happier conclusion to social progress; it was to share in Marcuse's vision of a "nonrepressive civilization" where mature, moral relations would flow from the fulfillment rather than from the repression of natural human passions.

In an effort to undo the link between morality and repression, Marcuse turned to a study of Freud and to an examination of what it was about human instincts that made Freud teach the inevitability of instinctual repression in society. In this kind of study of Freud, others soon followed—principally Norman O. Brown (*Life Against Death*), Philip Rieff (*Freud: The Mind of the Moralist*), Jürgen Habermas (*Knowledge and Human Interests*), and Paul Ricoeur (*Freud and Philosophy*). Through the efforts of such writers, Freud at long last took his rightful place at the center of moral and philosophical inquiry.

Today there is an impatience among scientific psychologists and practicing therapists with the philosopher in Freud. Basic parts of the psychoanalytic canon—for instance, Freud's speculations about a death instinct as the source of self-destructiveness or his mythologizing about prehistory—so obviously go beyond factual inquiry that science can regard them at best as irrelevancies, at worst as embarrassments. But it is often when Freud is at his most mythic and poetic that he grapples most powerfully with fundamental issues about human nature, about our loves and hates, our fondness for the light and yet our attractions to the dark. To read Freud is finally to have to ask, as a matter of values and not just facts, "Who am I?" and "What is the purpose of my life?"

Against the modern trend, therefore, this book is an essay in retrieval, an attempt to revive the discussion of Freud's implications for our moral, social, and political lives. But, of course, time does not stand still. The passion of youth for naturalness has meanwhile faded; with it has faded much of my own youthful enthusiasm for Marcuse's vision of a "nonrepressive civilization." My heart still feels the romance, but my head no longer comprehends the idea. The experience of studying Freud and writing this book has thus for me been an odyssey away from the book that set me on this journey long ago.

Nonetheless, I like to think that Marcuse would approve of the reading of Freud and of Freud's implications for freedom offered in this book. The modern sexual revolution, I argue, has delivered a considerable measure of freedom to contemporary men and women; we have successfully lifted so many of the damaging taboos on sexual activity or sexual diversity once thought inevitable. And yet, by approaching the question of freedom as if it were exclusively a matter of freedom *for* the individual *against* the community, we have achieved only a limited and partial kind of liberation. For, as Marcuse already saw in Freud, a liberated sexual lifestyle is never a matter of merely consuming other persons, one after the other, for the sake of bodily gratification alone. However much sexuality as a passion starts in this physical posture, it urges us on to form stable affections and enduring relations. To live a full erotic life is not to use and discard persons in a series of disconnected passions; it is to attain the enrichment and intensity of character that comes only from having lasting, passionate loyalties to family, to friends, and to fellow citizens—loyalties that shake, transform, and enlarge who we are. In other words, we do not need to repress our sexual and

LIBERATION
AND ITS LIMITS

LIBERATION AND ITS LIMITS

The Moral and Political Thought of Freud

Jeffrey B. Abramson

Beacon Press

Boston

Beacon Press
25 Beacon Street
Boston, Massachusetts 02108

Beacon Press books are published under the auspices
of the Unitarian Universalist Association
of Congregations in North America.

Copyright © 1984 by Jeffrey B. Abramson
Preface copyright © 1986 by Jeffrey B. Abramson

First published as a Beacon paperback in 1986 by arrangement
with The Free Press, a division of Macmillan, Inc.

All rights reserved

Printed in the United States of America

92 91 90 89 88 87 86   8 7 6 5 4 3 2 1

Library of Congress Cataloging in Publication Data

Abramson, Jeffrey B.
Liberation and its limits.

Reprint. Originally published: New York: Free
Press, © 1984.
Bibliography: p.
Includes index.
1. Freud, Sigmund, 1855–1939—Political and social
views.   2. Individuality.   3. Autonomy (Psychology)
4. Psychoanalysis.   I. Title.
BF173.F85A447   1986   150.19' 52   86–47551
ISBN 0–8070–2913–0 (pbk.)

To my parents
Albert and Rose Abramson

Contents

erotic drives to achieve lasting relations and common purposes with others; to the contrary, it is only in such relations and through such purposes that we grasp the erotic fulfillment we seek.

Much of what Freud nobly taught about health and happiness depends on his appreciation of this link between human eros and human sociability. And precisely because it is the liberation, not the repression, of eros that leads to the finest human relations, the vision of a future culture at peace with human nature can be kept alive and passed on to the next generation.

* * *

Over the many years I have been writing this book, I have been fortunate to receive the help of friends and teachers. There would have been no beginning without George Kateb, who first awakened me to political philosophy and taught me its necessity. By the force of her own example, Judith Shklar set me to work on disciplining my vision of freedom and to distinguishing argument from sentiment. Susan Moller Okin, Michael Rogin, and Jacqueline Jones all read earlier versions of the manuscript and gave me thoughtful comments that provoked much rewriting. My editor, Joyce Seltzer, gave invaluable encouragement and editorial assistance.

I owe a singular debt to Michael Sandel. Through the several drafts of this book, he has known, perhaps better than I did, what it was I was trying to say; he has helped me both to clarify my own views and also to change them under his always giving friendship and tutorship. At all times, he has supported my sense that Freud's vision of human liberation must be distinguished from the pale individualism dominant in our culture. To the extent that there is merit to the arguments about Freud and freedom in this book, I owe it to Michael's participation. He is in fact so deeply implicated in the substance of the argument that I happily can no longer make the author's standard claim of sole responsibility for his views.

My debt to my wife, Jacqueline Jones, and my daughters Sarah and Anna is not readily acknowledged, at least in public. Suffice it to say that a book on Freud which emphasizes the eros of community and the community of eros is first learned through the practice of family.

Waltham, Massachusetts
1986

Introduction:
Two Notions of Freedom

The ideal of the liberated self has become central to the moral vision of our age. "Find yourself"; "be yourself"; "be natural"; "get in touch with your feelings"—these are but some of the phrases testifying to the widespread contemporary equation of freedom with the value of self-expression. As against an older, republican tradition which identified freedom with public space, communal solidarity, and the activity of citizenship, freedom in modern society is most often envisioned as the personal achievement of individuals in private space—a matter of abolishing external constraints on the expression of one's inner or authentic self.

The relevance of other persons, or of politics in general, to freedom so conceived is not readily apparent. In the older, republican vision of freedom, political liberation was basic to personal liberation, because it was the community itself—and the public loyalties and virtues it spawned—that gave the self its character as well as its aims and purposes in life. By contrast, among ourselves it is the act of dispossessing the self of community, of tradition and religion and family, that is commonly seen as therapeutic and liberating.

Freud's influence on contemporary aspirations for liberation is broad and secure. And yet his moral vision of the free self has not, I think, been adequately understood or pursued. According to the prevailing interpretation of psychoanalysis, Freud's teachings are profoundly anticommunity and radically individualist. Freud stands against community, in this view, because he dismissed almost all forms of group allegiance as curious, sometimes dangerous, attempts to console man the infant for the harshness of reality. According to this reading, furthermore, Freud preferred the psychology of alienation over the loyalties bred by either religion or politics. And for modern alienated men and women, Freud is preeminently known for devising a new therapy—an intense, private, and indwelling form of liberation in which one finds freedom and well-being only by becoming, in Philip Rieff's term, a "virtuoso of the self." Such a virtuoso is at once radically knowledgeable about the origin of his or her own desires, unburdened of moral constraints that cannot survive negotiation with reason, and situated in the world no longer by reference to gods or traditions, but solely in terms of what science can reveal about who one is.

If this dominant reading of Freud were correct, then psychoanalysis would provide considerable support for our reigning notions about freedom and privacy. But while there is obviously much in Freud's writings that resonates with those quests for liberation that focus on the isolated self, I will argue in this book for a second, more adequate reading through which Freud can be seen as contributing to a more communitarian vision of liberation and well-being. He does this by setting out in unsurpassed manner the limits to the competing, atomized understanding of liberation. Freud foresaw and criticized the modern appeal of an ethic of self-assertion and spontaneity, an ethic that has roots in Nietzsche but parades today under the banners of the permissive society and sexual liberation. Against any such easy understanding of liberty as license for naturalness and self-expression, Freud explored the internal contradictions of erotic life and repeatedly and bleakly emphasized the incompleteness of the kind of liberation we can achieve merely by "living out" desire. To take Freud and psychoanalysis seriously, therefore, is to conclude that much of what passes for liberation in contemporary society is empty—individualism run riot, as it were. Psychoanalysis is in fact one of the gravest moral indictments our culture has known. This was true of the judgment Freud levied against his own supposedly repressive culture. But it is true also about the judgment psychoanalysis demands of our own sexual "liberation."

Nor is Freud's critical distance from the radically individualist and self-expressive therapy underlying the platform of the permissive society limited to sexual matters. The prevailing reading of Freud tends to obscure the extent to which psychoanalysis is an "intersubjective" science of the mind—a distinctive study of how the child's ego is constituted and enriched by attachments to others, attachments deep enough to enter into who the child is becoming. In the key psychoanalytic theory of identification, Freud explores just how precarious personal identity is, how unstable the boundaries between distant selves. This vulnerability of personality can be for better or worse. Freud himself characteristically worried about the sinister forms politics and religion take when the sense of distance between persons collapses. But Freud's account of moral development in children also shows that, apart from deep attachments to others, the self is left impoverished, unable to experience the friendships and loyalties that enrich personal character.

Of course, Freud did not often talk directly about politics and freedom. His immediate concern, both as clinician and theorist, was with the tension between repression and expression of human instinctuality, and it is here that we must expect to find clues to his moral vision. Fortunately, the pioneering work of Marcuse and Rieff, among others,[1] has long since made clear just how politically important Freud's exploration of human instinctuality is, and I propose to follow their work in arguing in particular about Eros, politics, and freedom, as follows.

Freud conceived of Eros as basic to the human condition and sexuality as basic to Eros. But from infancy onward, Eros becomes fused with and compromised by the equally strong human instinct for destruction. So alloyed with aggression, Freudian Eros becomes as much a process of self-estrangement as self-fulfillment. Self and other in love are for Freud also self and other involved in a contest for power and mastery. Indeed, whatever love one has to give to the other (Freud's category of "object-love") is apparently at the expense of what remains for self-love. These antagonisms within affection are present even or perhaps especially in the family, and a central theme of psychoanalysis is the drama whereby children come to repress their own erotic strivings and aggressive hostilities in favor of a fearful submission to the parent. Indeed, instead of being a vehicle for liberation, Eros becomes the source of a moral conscience whose commandments are strangely self-violent and repressive, as if the child had deflected his hostile urges away from the beloved parent and onto his unworthy self.

Freud's account of the dilemma of human nature caught between erotic and cruel inclinations is powerful and has showered illumination on aspects of childhood that, while dimly perceived
prior to psychoanalysis, never seemed so terribly formative, so
fraught with destiny. It is also that part of the psychoanalytic canon
which is responsible for the widely held view that Freud followed
Hobbes in portraying all human relations as, at base, forms of antagonism. Such a reading of Freud must be given its due; Freud's
dominant account of Eros is indeed gloomy, and the Oedipus complex gives symbolic summary to the aggressive underbelly of even
our closest relationships.

But Freud is not just a latter-day Hobbes, and I will argue that,
at least at times, he speaks of Eros and human attachment with a
more affirmative, less dire voice. It is in this voice that Freud speaks
of the "highest erotic bliss of childhood"; and when Freud con-
cretely describes the relation between infant and mother, he
describes, against his own theoretical animus, a moment of union,
or being at one with the other, that enriches the identity of both
without impoverishing either. In the act of nursing, for instance,
the mother gives of herself for the pleasure of her child. But it is
only by so giving to the pleasure of another that the mother experiences her own pleasure *as* a mother, her own enrichment and
enlargement of character. In other words, her self-fulfillment is
hardly in tension with, but is in fact dependent on, fulfilling the
other as well.

On a more theoretical level, when Freud reformulated his
theory of instincts late in his career, he specifically jettisoned an
earlier, more solipsistic description of the aims of the sexual instinct in favor of a direct definition of Eros as the drive for union
with the other. This theoretical elevation of the human desire for
union was prepared for by a lifetime's clinical study of the frequency with which human dreams and fantasies turn on images of
incorporating or being incorporated into another human being
(usually the mother). Alongside his Hobbesian pessimism about
the integrity of human attachments, therefore, Freud also affirmed
in part the career of Eros beyond antagonism, thereby keeping
alive within psychoanalysis mankind's most utopian aspirations.

Still, as opposed to the tradition of moral and political
philosophy which linked rather than opposed community and
freedom, Freud never went on to give any sustained attention to
the public forms erotic attachments might assume outside the

family—in friendship centrally and citizenship occasionally. But to see that such allegiances at least sometimes wear an erotic face is to see, in accord with the older tradition of liberation, that Eros potentially sponsors political attachments between persons who see themselves as sharing in a common identity as citizens. The aspiration to a public life answering to, rather than repressive of, Eros is therefore a worthy moral and political ideal, but it can be gestured toward only by allowing, perhaps more than Freud himself did, for the fundamental difference between the reciprocity of erotic relations and the dominations of power.

After offering an overview of the problem of Eros and politics in Chapter One, I will set forth Freud's explicit psychology of love, attempting to cull from it an affirmative teaching regarding the "happy love" achieved by children through the extremity of their dependence on the parents. The basis for this reading is provided by the concept of identification and the intersubjective process whereby the child comes to have a first and "oceanic" sense of self by reference to the image or model of the parents. Such a notion of how an ego is constituted so as to "be like" the beloved parents is suggestive of attachments beyond the rooted antagonisms of which Freud characteristically speaks.

But an ambivalence of love and hate is the rule even in early infancy, and hence the "efflorescence" of infantile Eros is "doomed to extinction." Freud proceeds to document the sinister and self-repressive uses to which identification with the other is put in order to control human aggression. The tracing of Freud's pessimism in this regard will take us through Chapter Five.

On the level of therapy, Freud's affirmative voice is heard more often. Starting with the ethic of sublimation, Freud offers a partial "way out of" the predominance of self-repressive psychology. Eros, according to Freud, can be "desexualized" and rechanneled into public and civil affections that are nonetheless compensatory forms of individual gratification. But this process of sublimation remains shadowy in psychoanalysis, not the least because desexualization threatens to atrophy the force of Eros and tilt the always precarious instinctual balance in favor of destruction. Moreover, Freud's commitment to sublimation is qualified by his refusal to follow the Platonic account of sublimation and allow desire to take on the qualities and virtues of the object it loves. Instead, Freud rejects Plato's familiar distinction between "higher and lower" pleasures in favor of the persistence of the infantile essence of desire throughout a life history. These criticisms of sublimation will form the substance of Chapter Six.

Nonetheless, the concept of sublimation does point toward the limited personal liberation Freud thought he could deliver to his patients in therapy. If the survival of infantile desire over time gives to every life history a regressive potential, it also makes that life history tell an intelligible story, at least in retrospect. Through the recollection of origins, we come to comprehend the destiny of character as it has been fixed so far by the circumstances of childhood. But such an act of self-apprehension is itself a further moment in the unfolding of the life history being understood, a new piece of the character that constitutes our fate. Indeed, as I will argue in Chapter Seven, psychoanalysis as therapy stands or falls with the claim that human beings, unlike other natural objects, can understand themselves in ways that henceforth change what there was to be understood.

Psychoanalytic freedom lies, then, not in some desublimating ethic of immediate "self-expression" or sexual liberation or Reichian living out of repressed desire. It lies in the slow and gradual process of self-understanding which alone gives access to and mastery over primitive experience. "Where id was, ego shall be." And Freud conceived of this act of mastery primarily as a process of distancing oneself from the hold of the past, an undoing of the fate one has been living and of the arrests in development that come from keeping mind ignorant of its own origins.

But once the past is dispossessed of its power over mental life, the psychoanalytic project of liberation has evidently reached its limits. Psychoanalysis is not, Freud remarked, psychosynthesis. It has no *Weltanschauung,* or world view, and suggests no new meaning for a life suddenly disenchanted of its former sense of purpose and meaning. Freud rightly sensed that through psychoanalysis science had won a decisive victory over religion, thereby rendering unstable the most widely held answers to the meaning of life. What did science have to offer in place? What new set of moral beliefs could the analyzed self affirm in the absence of God? What new erotic attachments could be formed by one who comprehended the longing for the parent which had hitherto dictated all choices in love? To what form of political life or community could one pledge rational allegiance once the need of the infant within the citizen for consolation and proxy father figures had been exposed? These are some of the questions of psychosynthesis which Freud refused to answer but which must guide the attempt to reunderstand morality and politics in the light of perhaps the most important commentary penned on the human condition in this century.

_____ *Chapter One* _____

Eros and Politics

Psychoanalysis precariously holds together two rival teachings about human nature and culture. The first, more accessible teaching declares the tragic opposition between instinct and culture, and culminates in *Civilization and Its Discontents'* well-known argument that culture tames nature only through a painful, often ruthless process of external frustration and suppression. The second, more hidden and central testament of psychoanalysis is to the essential sociability of human nature—the primal need, present already in infants, for the love, affection, and company of others. This account of civility before culture culminates in the notion of an Oedipus complex and a saga of the *self*-repressions upon which all later authority is based.

I

Freud develops his account of nature *against* culture by locating the human animal in a natural history of desire, with origins in bodily urges of a most unruly and anarchic sort. To lift the veil on self-reflection imposed by infantile amnesia is to learn dark secrets about the animal core of desire and its uneasy humanization. In Freud's final view, human nature is torn between two opposing forces: an instinct for life, called Eros, which aims at uniting life forms together and preserving their existence; and an instinct for death and destruction, which aims at dissolving life back into the primeval inertness of inorganic matter.[1] Culture's pacification of the destructive urge is at the center of Freud's tragic vision, because the gloomy choice is between destruction expended against self *or* other. The "cultural" solution is to internalize aggression as self-destruction, and this accounts at base for the "tormenting uneasiness" of civilized life.[2]

Culture's confrontation with Eros, while not equally doomed for Freud, is nonetheless rife with tensions between private and public pleasures, individual gratification and "aim-inhibited" social relationships. Sexuality in particular is an unruly, asocial passion, by nature a rebellion against the conventions of normality, and capable of every sort of sadism and violence, perversion and transgression against order. Freud's account of infantile sexuality in particular drives home one point repeatedly—naturally Eros knows no principle of organization; it is a pure anarchy of bodily pleasures, or, as Freud puts it, "polymorphous perversity."[3]

Just *how* disorderly sexuality is as a passion we commonly miss due to the absurdly narrow custom of restricting the label of sexuality to the already organized, contained, and functional sensations of the "sexual" (i.e., genital) organs.[4] But even the popular view of sexuality cannot abide by its own conventions. It must acknowledge that some persons experience undeniably sexual excitement in so-called perverse, or nongenital, ways. And it must further allow that such perverse eroticism plays a role (albeit a subsidiary one) in even normal sexual stimulation.

When the psychoanalysis of neurosis shows that perversions are not just "rarities" or "oddities" but deviate from conventional behavior only in the sense of returning to infantile bodily gratifications we all once experienced, then the discomfort of the popular view is complete.[5] The use of the conventions of normality to mask the animal truth is exposed and nature reveals itself in all its radical asociability. In Freud's terms, we then discover infantile sexuality to be a loosely connected set of "component" instincts, with no image of the body as a whole, no stable aim or object, finding "organ pleasure" in every corner and crevice of the body.[6] Such an Eros, it would seem, has no internal limits or sociability; it must be perpetually narrowed, organized, and restrained by outside sources. Eros may be a Roman cupid, a playful child, but the child plays with arrows.

But the above sketch of nature versus culture does not exhaust Freud's vision. In fact, as both Rieff and Marcuse suggest, psychoanalysis is a powerful retort to the natural man/social man tension that has dominated political philosophy from and after Hobbes. For what Freud characteristically insists upon is that, already within the state of nature and the unrepressed desires of childhood, Eros takes the form not only of anarchic pleasure striving but also of a deep emotional need for the company of others, for the love and protection of the parents. The dilemma of childhood, put simply, is that this need to be loved stands threatened by the contrary aggressive impulses the child also entertains toward the loved parents, a dilemma which eventually coheres into the Oedipal fantasies of sexual rebellion against the loved and hated parental rival. But what Freud defines as the passing or dissolution of the Oedipal complex is the triumph of love over hate, the submission to and internalization of parental authority as the child's own conscience, or superego. This loving identification with the parent henceforth mutes the outer expressions of rebellion and harnesses aggression to the self.

Freud was pursued throughout his career by the Rousseauist criticism that he conflated the social with the natural by reading back the work of family association into the structure of instinct. Freud made his defense by referring to the evolutionary history Eros has even on the level of instinct. To imagine, with Rousseau, a prehistory of Eros prior to all stable human attachments is to imagine away the organic and biological changes that have accompanied and accomplished the speciation of humans.[7] For ever since the human animal stood upright and revealed its genitals, sexuality has been a permanent rather than a periodic urge, and man has been a "horde" animal.[8] The Eros we can know as humans therefore is a passion that is structured from the beginning by the family as a society. And every family, over and above cultural differences, will enact the core of the Oedipal dilemma: a rebellious appropriation of parents as sex objects; a deferential surrender of that rebellion, out of fear and need of the parents.

II

Politics for Freud continues the Oedipal longing for love and authority and the consoling search for dependence on new father figures. In the state-of-nature theory popularized by Hobbes and Locke, the self is seen as fully formed outside of society, persuaded into political community only as the better device for protecting private space from the anticipated but unwanted encroachments of others. Freud's understanding of the ambition of politics is fundamentally different, here more like Rousseau in seeing in politics a vast remolding of an unstable self seeking the company of others to complete itself, possessed by a need to diminish distance between self and other. At bottom, therefore, politics counts on an attraction and obedience that is erotic and nonrational in nature, a redirection of emotions previously reserved for the family toward the state. Freud thus refers to the "libidinal constitution" of groups and notes that if

> an individual gives up his distinctiveness in a group . . . , it gives one the impression that he does it because he feels the need of being in harmony with them rather than in opposition to them—so that perhaps after all he does it *"ihnen zu Liebe"* [for love of them].[9]

This vision of politics as a sphere of love has a long and ambiguous history in Western political thought. A chasm separates those who have seen in eroticized politics the most alluring of utopias and those who have regarded it as the most totalitarian of possibilities. Plato's *Republic* remains a sounding board against which to state one's position. In the *Republic* Plato proposes to extend the ties of kinship love into the public sphere by raising a class of future rulers in ignorance of blood parentage, each member calling all contemporaries by the name of brother and sister and all elders by the name of mother or father. For such persons, the difference between family feeling and public loyalty will have collapsed. The life they hold in common will be the only "private" life they know, and hence "each shares in a common interest which each will call his own."[10] Outside of the construction of such a common life, Plato conceived of Eros as a grave danger to political order, a "great winged drone" stinging the soul into the tyrannical assertion of its own insatiable appetites. It takes, therefore, the establishment of a certain sort of community, where public allegiance replaces kinship loyalty and self-love, for Eros to become a source of unity rather than division.

The utopian dimension of the *Republic* has been met with two fundamentally different kinds of arguments through the history of political philosophy. The first dissents from love as essentially a *prepolitical* passion which cannot withstand publicity and disappears when made universal. The second recoils from love as the most *antipolitical* of passions, which perverts not only its own nature when dragged out into the light of day, but also the nature of politics and the core virtues upon which public as opposed to private life depends: space, distance, respect, reason, and light.

The prepolitical response to Platonic Eros was made decisively by Aristotle. Aristotle shared with Plato a vision of the *polis* as a good life in common, a shared identity, and a sphere of a certain kind of friendship. But he insisted against Plato that politics was a realm qualitatively different from private life, unable to duplicate either the virtues or warmth of the family. To attempt to extend kinship ties into the public arena was to end up with only a weak and watery kind of metaphorical familiarity:

> What is common to the greatest number gets the least amount of care. Men pay most attention to what is their own. They care less for what is common or, at any rate, they care for it only to the extent to which each is individually concerned.... The scheme of Plato means that each citizen will have a thousand sons; they will not be the sons of each citizen individually: any and every son will be equally the son of any and every father; and the result will be that every son will be equally neglected by every father.[11]

This argument that love, however fine a passion in private, is simply too weak to inform a wider set of public relations, comprises a recurring motif in Western philosophy. Hume, for instance, notes the obstacles to extrapolating the natural sentiments of family life into politics and the consequent need to make do with the "distant" and "artificial" sentiment we call justice.[12] More recently Popper has expressed the prepolitics of love as follows:

> [W]e cannot feel the same emotions towards everybody. Emotionally, we all divide men into those who are near to us, and those who are far from us.... We cannot really love "in the abstract"; we can love only those whom we know. Thus the appeal even to our best emotions, love and compassion, can only tend to divide mankind into different categories.[13]

The second argument—concerning the antipolitics of Eros—takes the *Republic* and its utopian progeny to task in a more vehement manner. Politics alloyed with love destroys love, first of all, because it no longer tolerates the private space and hidden recesses upon which love's intimacy depends. Every love relation becomes a matter of public concern, a potential rival to the forging of common allegiances and public loyalties. So publicized and scrutinized, love is no longer recognizable. Indeed, to practice the politics of Eros is to follow Plato, and Rousseau and Fourier after him, in distrusting love's privatizing trend above all else. Eros is politically useful only when manipulated and mutilated under the all-seeing eye of Big Brother.

At the same time, this criticism continues, love made public destroys politics and the concept of public space.[14] When politics concerns itself with the intimate passions, it takes up residence in the dark and shadows. The boundaries traditionally imposed on the political agenda by notions of privacy are traded for the privileged collapse of space between lovers. Thus, the argument goes, political Eros, however alluring, is the inevitable precursor of totalitarianism and the eradication of the difference between public and private life. Politics lodges itself in the most intimate recesses of life as love without restraint:

> [T]here are a great many things which cannot withstand the implacable, bright light of the constant presence of others on the public scene, . . . which can survive only in the realm of the private. For instance, love, in distinction from friendship, is killed or rather extinguished, the moment it is displayed in public. ("Never seek to tell thy love / Love that never told can be.") Because of its inherent worldlessness, love can only become false and perverted when it is used for political purposes such as the change or salvation of the world.[15]

III

Freud's views on politics and love have been subject to contrary interpretations. He has been read, most notably by Rieff, as offering a bleak vision of the sinister power produced from their unfortunate mixture.[16] In this view, Freud is politically a defender of liberal distance between persons—of freedom as independence. Love thus implicitly threatens enlightened politics because it is in tension with the maintenance of the distinctiveness of the individual. Freud recognized of course that most persons crave a cozier sort of community, but he chided man the infant for everywhere enchaining himself to the politics of consolation or the religion of salvation.

In this reading, Freud's mistrust of politics' alliance with love is more a matter of the antipolitics than the prepolitics of love. Freud makes the prepolitical arguments, most especially against the "absurd" universalism of Christian love:

> [I]f I am to love him (with this universal love) merely because he, too, is an inhabitant of this earth, like an insect, an earth-worm or a grass-snake, then I fear that only a small modicum of my love will fall to his share. . . . [17]

But love against politics seems his special viewpoint. Against Hume's observation that politics cannot be family life writ large, Freud feared that love not only can but will reach the political sphere, bringing into public life all the unfinished business of rebellion and submission in the family.

Despite this bleakness, Freud has also been read, most notably by Marcuse, as suggesting a hidden optimism about politics and Eros. As we have seen, in Freud's final instinct theory Eros is a "ceaseless trend" toward the unification of persons; it is a will to live which Freud repeatedly compares to "Eros of the divine Plato" in order to capture the continuity of desire from its instinctual-sexual forms to its inhibited or sublime manifestations.[18] Through the early years of his career, Freud attended mostly to the isolating inner life of fantasy spun out by Eros in response to social frustration. But to offer a psychology of what makes humans human after all is to attend to the life that mind leads in culture as well as in the unconscious.[19] And in the five books and several papers which constitute Freud's return to his youthful interest in cultural problems, psychoanalytic Eros becomes an affirmative force for culture, opposing the disturbances of the death instinct and orienting persons to the gratifications that come only from being bound to the other. Of course, the finite amount of energy men and women have at their disposal means that a politics of Eros will trigger its share of disputes over the distribution of Eros between individual and society. But we shall see that Freud himself was far from considering this tension to be tragic. It admits of "eventual accommodation."

It is not the purpose of this book to render a belated verdict as between these two visions of Freud's approach to Eros, each of which has powerfully illumined aspects of psychoanalysis. I wish instead to approach the question of politics and Eros from the perspective that seems most basic to Freud—that of the primal ambivalence in human nature between Eros and death. The only Eros we typically know, according to Freud, is one already partly estranged from the desire for union, and perverted by a hidden alliance with the destructive energy of the death instinct. This Eros calls forth the Oedipal dilemma of love versus hate and ends in the self-tormenting surrender to the parent that makes the infantile relation between love and authority a troublesome model for politics.

Any fair reading of Freud must attend to this irreconcilable conflict between Eros and death darkening all human attachments from family to state. There is no psychoanalysis without the hypothesis of an inner instinctual conflict from which humanity can never fully escape—except by going over entirely to the death instinct. But there is also no psychoanalysis without an affirmation of the ability of Eros to hold the balance of power over death. This affirmation is fragile, the more so since

> [m]en have gained control over the forces of nature to such an extent that with their help they would have no difficulty in exterminating one another to the last man.[20]

But now

> it is to be expected that the other of the two "Heavenly Powers," eternal Eros, will make an effort to assert himself in the struggle with his equally immortal adversary.[21]

How Eros asserts itself against aggression and at what costs comprises the heart of Freud's political psychology. That politics must lean heavily on Eros, must indeed exaggerate public affection between persons so as to stave off the counterforce of aggression, makes politicized Eros both an enemy and ally of human freedom. An enemy, because whenever the boundaries between separate selves prove politically movable, the opportunity for manipulation of personality is present. An ally, because only when personality is at risk in politics, as it is in love, can personal character be completed by the virtues born of public activity.

Traditionally, liberal societies have opposed the closing of distance between persons that erotic politics portends. In the name of individual autonomy, liberalism has sought instead to secure public respect for the distinctiveness of each individual life and for the limits of public concern with private life. But when the distinction between separate selves is maintained so firmly as to empty politics of its ability to foster shared purposes and common goals, then liberation reaches its limit.

Chapter Two

Eros and the
Psychology of Love

Eros, according to Freud, pursues two kinds of attachments in the world—"object love," or the desire to have another person; and "identification," or the desire to be like another.[1] But what is it we want to possess in the beloved? And whom do we wish to be like? Freud sought the answer to these questions in the infantile origins of desire and in the prehistory that burdens and partly defines adult love's agenda.

I

In describing the path taken by "object-love," Freud begins with what he takes to be the earliest form in which Eros awakens to interest in an external object: the sensual pleasure the infant experiences in the act of gaining nourishment at the breast. Freud describes this stage as "anaclitic sexuality," meaning literally sexuality "leaning up against" the self-preservative urge to suck for survival.[2] That is to say, biological need selects out the breast (or some substitute) as the first external object to which the infant gropes. But from "the very beginning," suckling has an erotic as

well as self-preservative moment.[3] Thus Freud can say that the
breast comprises the infant's first choice of a sexual object—the
prototypical appropriation of the other as a source of one's own
gratification.[4]

In the earliest stage of this object relation, the external location
of the breast is not comprehended and the infant acts as if it could
"devour" or "assimilate" into itself the source of pleasure.[5] But as
the infant increasingly apprehends its dependency on an object
outside itself, the possessive aim of anaclitic sexuality becomes anx-
iously transparent:

> An infant at the breast does not as yet distinguish his ego from the ex-
> ternal world as the source of the sensations flowing in upon him. He
> gradually learns to do so . . . recogniz[ing] [that] his own bodily
> organs. . . can provide him with sensations at any moment, whereas
> other sources evade him from time to time—among them what he de-
> sires most of all, his mother's breast—and only reappear as a result of
> his screaming for help.[6]

Freud allows that children also form object relations to the
father, but he tended to view this as a later development, having to
do with the (eventually more formidable) need for protection and
not tending. At any rate, whether as a desire for motherly care or
fatherly protection, the sexual relation to an object one also needs
merely to stay alive cannot help but be radically grasping. However
intense the bond between infant and mother at the breast, the attachment could at first be described as that of a parasite in need.
The infant seems unawake to and unrestrained by appreciation of
the parent as a differentiated other.

The doubling of self-preservative objects as sexual objects
passes as the child substitutes an anarchy of autoerotic satisfactions
for the primal choice of the breast. Sexuality comes into a life of its
own, a remarkable and privileged internal feeding on the joy of
one's own body. But in his study of dreams and neuroses, Freud
concluded that the original object relation to the mother at the
breast is never entirely sundered. Mankind is uneasily weaned from
its paradigmatic experience of gratification, and thumb sucking is
typical of a pattern of substitute gratification. This, I take it, is the
meaning of Freud's cryptic remark, "a child sucking at his
mother's breast has become the prototype of every relation of love.
The finding of an object is in fact a refinding of it."[7]

But if the finding of love for adults is always the refinding of infantile love, then object-love is always partly the possession of the wrong person—the proxy for the parent upon whom desire is unconsciously fixed. To uncover the hidden motives of object-love is thus to threaten its stability. A person may love

> [a]ccording to the anaclitic. . .type:
>   (a) the woman who feeds him,
>   (b) the man who protects him,
> and the *succession of substitutes who take their place*.[8] (Emphasis added.)

Such needy origins make Freudian object-love reminiscent of Socrates' description in the *Symposium* of Eros as born of the self's sense of defect and the consequent drive to appropriate the other to complete oneself. But Socrates was prepared to affirm the ethical triumph over need implicit in the lover's sense of incompleteness and the creative urge to redraw the deficient self after the image of the beautiful and good in the other. Freud made no parallel affirmation because adult love can never appropriate or unite with the right person, can never address the real sense of loss. Indeed, what makes object-love unstable in Freud's view is that the attempt to appropriate the other to satisfy inner needs leads only to a vast impoverishment. The beloved is deemed the possessor of all perfections, which by comparison the lover lacks:

> Complete object-love of the [anaclitic] type . . . displays . . . marked sexual overvaluation. . . . This sexual overvaluation is the origin of the peculiar state of being in love, a state suggestive of a neurotic compulsion, which is thus traceable to an impoverishment of the ego as regards libido in favour of the love-object.[9]

Thus there is more to Freud's insight into the structure of possessive love than the conventional point about the way in which need for another person often translates into an urge to dominate that person. Freud's deeper insight is that object-love is always partly a form of self-desertion. It is an exaltation of the other as the possessor of all one is not, the embodiment of the ideal. This is why Freud often compared being in love to being hypnotized.[10]

II

Freud used his central insight into object-love's attempts at regaining the parent to explain the frequency of sexual difficulties within modern marriage. "Where [persons] love they do not desire and where they desire they cannot love."[11] The former dissociation leads to frigidity or psychical impotence, difficulties Freud considered far more widespread than conventional opinion allows.[12] The latter division produces "a special type object choice made by men"—the choice exclusively of "fallen women" as sexual objects.[13]

Why love and sexuality should commonly go their separate ways is not immediately obvious. After all, Freud noted in his *Contributions to the Psychology of Love,* for a "completely normal attitude in love" to emerge, "[t]wo currents of [feeling have to unite]. These two may be distinguished as the *affectionate* and the *sensual* current."[14]

But disunion is more common than convergence for the following reasons. Of the two currents of love, affection "is the older," springing up from the very "earliest years of childhood" in gratitude to those who have care of the child.[15] The sexual current, as we have seen, is "anaclitic" to this original affectionate tie, and thus "from the very beginning," the objects upon whom the child depends and to whom he returns affection are at the same time objects of sexual choice and gratification. Thus we can speak of the convergence of sensuality and affection in early childhood. But affection is a deep anchor, fixed on the parental relation through childhood and absorbing erotic elements, which are thus "diverted from . . . sexual aims."[16] This process of sensuality empowering the infant-parent relation continues until the transformations of puberty make the direct sexual aim no longer disguisable. Barred from satisfaction within the family by the intervening incest taboo, the sensual current thus seeks satisfaction in the outer world in relation to persons "chosen on the model (imago)" of the parents.[17] Normal love results to the extent that this proxy relation can pull up the anchor of affection from its parental moorings and rechannel the tender current into sexual life.

However, two obstacles stand in the way of such a happy resolution to object-love. The first concerns "the amount of frustration in reality" which the sensual current meets. To the extent that culture suppresses sexual opportunity from without, the current is dammed and turned backward toward infantile patterns. Freud thought such cultural deprivation an important contributing factor in the modern sexual malaise and its neurotic results.[18] But there is a deeper cause of the schism between love and desire, compared to which external frustration functions only as a "triggering cause" in psychoanalytic theory.[19] This second problem lies in "the amount of *attraction*" that may be exercised by the infantile objects [the parents] themselves.[20] This unsurrendered but unconscious incestuous fixation predisposes persons, in varying degrees, to find adult love unsatisfying, an experience for which not all of their libido is available.

If the infantile attractions all along or as later reawakened by cultural frustration prove powerful enough, then "libido turns away from reality, . . . strengthens the images of the first sexual objects and becomes fixated to them."[21] Of course, the incest barrier most often insists that such revived infantilism should remain repressed and unconscious, absorbed into fantasy or neurotic symptoms. If the entire current is so absorbed, then total impotence or frigidity results. Far more common among Freud's patients, however, was what he called "psychical" impotence or frigidity. Here, a person is able to experience both love and sex with other persons but never with the same person. One loves those who, for one reason or another, are fit to serve as parental proxies. But to have sex with parental proxies comes too close to reviving the repressed incestuous desire for the parents themselves. Hence the recurrent dualism Freud saw in his patients' lives: love without sexual satisfaction in marriage and sex without love outside of marriage.

It is sometimes suggested that psychoanalysis is partly dated, since its theories reflect life before the "sexual revolution." But Freud's claim about Victorian society was never the crude and inaccurate one that men and women suffered from not having enough sex. He diagnosed the less technical, more mental difficulty of holding together desire and affection, and it is far from obvious that the sexual revolution has healed the divorce to which Freud addressed himself. Indeed, insofar as the modern permissive society alleges the curative effects of "living out" desire, it is what Freud dismissed as "wild psychoanalysis."

III

Contributions to the Psychology of Love makes clear that Freudian object-love is at best a precarious venture in liberation, mired in trying to have in the other a substitute satisfaction for what one really wants and cannot have: an incestuous object choice.

   In his powerfully illuminating, but I think partial commentary
on these papers, Rieff puts forward the following interpretation of
Freud's sense of love's inability to free itself from the hold of the
past.[22] Since Freud refers to affection as "older" than sensuality, it
cannot be just its sublimation, as commentators and Freud himself
sometimes assume. Instead, the "dilemma of our emotional lives"
is set by the priority of affection, by the fact that the primary form
of love is "authoritarian," a child's "compliant and grateful
response to parental dominance."[23] Liberation is an odyssey away
from such submission, but love is partly an obstacle to freedom,
due to its tendency to arrest the sensual current and fixate it upon
the first relation to authority. Repeatedly Rieff describes the child's
affection for its parents as a love of "authority." Infantile love is
"tender" and "compliant."[24] It is a model instance of "submission," an "insatiable love of authority–figures."[25] But this
authority-laden terminology is penned by Rieff, not Freud. The insight gained by interpreting, in terms of domination and submission, what Freud does say about infants and parents is, of course,
considerable. Rieff's account brings to the fore what, by any
reading, is a key aspect of psychoanalysis: the *self*-repression
generated by a child fearful of the loss of parental love and protection. But however illuminating Rieff is in this regard, there are still
grounds for suspecting that the description of love as
"authoritarian" by " 'nature' (that is, originally)"[26] is only a partial account of Freud's teaching. Rieff derives the submissive
nature of love from the infant's gratitude to the all-protecting
parent.[27] But Freud typically spoke of the infant's ambivalence, not
gratitude, which Rieff himself insists upon elsewhere ("the . . .
law of primal ambivalence").[28] The infant's emotional tie to its
parents, Freud noted, is "ambivalent from the very first; it can
turn into an expression of tenderness as easily as into a wish for
someone's removal."[29]
   Indeed, Freud proposes the remarkable notion that love and
hate coexist in the child's earliest object relations. "Originally, at
the very beginning of mental life," the infantile ego is indifferent
to the external world, absorbed in what Freud calls the "happy
love" of taking itself as its only love object.[30] When this state is
disturbed by the stimuli of the external world and libido must be
withdrawn from the ego and invested in attending to objects, there
is the dual reaction of hate and love, with hate being the "older
reaction," the attempt to negate the source of disturbance:

[I]t cannot be denied that hating . . . originally characterized the relation of the ego to the alien external world with the stimuli it introduces.
Indifference falls into place as a special case of hate or dislike, after having first appeared as their forerunner. At the very beginning, it seems,
the external world, objects and what is hated are identical.[31]

Love is a later achievement, accomplished only when the object
proves itself as a source of pleasure as well as tension, something
that the ego strives to bring nearer to itself, indeed to "incorporate" into itself.

In tune with this admixture of hateful and loving responses to
the pains and pleasures of external reality, Freud speaks of the
infant-parent tie not only as "compliant" and "grateful" but also
as "hostile" and "aggressive." "Not until the genital organization is established does love become the opposite of hate." [32] In the
oral stage typified by sucking at the breast, the admixture of love
and hate is testified to by a relation to the breast Freud refers to as a
"devouring affection"—an impulse to swallow, incorporate, in-
troduce, or introject the object into the ego, thereby annihilating
it.[33] In the anal stage, "the striving for the object appears in the
form of an urge for mastery, to which injury or annihilation of the
object is a matter of indifference." This form and preliminary
stage of love "is hardly to be distinguished from hate in its attitude
towards the object." [34]

Freud's description of the early infant-parent tie is therefore
nowhere near as tame as the remark about the priority of affection
in the *Contributions to the Psychology of Love* taken by itself
might imply. We shall see that, by introducing the concept of a
primal instinct for death and self-destructiveness, Freud brought
the child's ambivalence between love and hate to the very center of
psychoanalytic theory. But even prior to postulating a separate
destructive urge, Freud sensed that the infant's relation to the
parent is an anarchic confusion of rebellion and submission, civility
and disorder, aggression and affection. Rieff's insistence that "by
nature" love is authoritarian thus flattens out Freud's moral tale
and obscures what again Rieff himself highlights: the drama of
conflict presented by Oedipal psychology and the repressions it
takes to make a child compliant.

There is a further and deeper difficulty with any description of
the infant-parent tie as authoritarian. Rieff presents a Freud for
whom dependencies are all of one sort: hierarchical relations in
which one person dominates and the other submits. Much is at

stake here for theories of liberation, insofar as Rieff's Freud calls into question the differences we commonly insist upon between the reciprocity of love and the coercions of power. Indeed, love becomes the most dominating means of socialization because it is the most internal. That Freud must be at least partly understood along Rieff's line of interpretation is beyond dispute. But both clinically and theoretically, Freud moved toward positions in his later writings which affirm liberating potential in love beyond the rooted antagonism of one self dominating over or submitting to the other.

Theoretically, Freud reformulated an earlier, conflictual view of sexuality as an urge to use the other only to reduce the level of painful tension inside oneself in favor of a less isolating, more expansive Eros. This Eros is a basic drive *for* unification; it takes pleasure even in the tension that comes from extending oneself toward the other.[35] Clinically, Freud became increasingly committed to the formative importance of the primal aim of union with the mother, preceding the father love which controls the Oedipus complex. He compared his surprise at this deeper layer of psychology to that which must have been experienced by archaeologists upon "the discovery of the Minoan-Mycenaean civilization behind that of Greece."[36]

Freud's description of the infant at the mother's breast is not romantic or "preambivalent," as some commentators have interpreted it.[37] Even here, he detects urges to devour on the one hand, fears of being devoured on the other. But if the primal relation of baby to mother should not be unduly romanticized, neither should it be described as authoritarian in Rieff's sense or indeed possessive according to Freud's own definition of object-love. Instead, what Freud describes is a desire on the part of the infantile ego to overcome the anxiety-provoking separation from the source of its gratification, to incorporate and not merely distantly appropriate the body which gives it pleasure. In other words, the aim of infantile Eros is union with the mother's body not as other, but as integral to its own self-fulfillment. In terms such as "incorporation," "introjection," and "assimilation," Freud appears to strive toward an intersubjective-sounding vocabulary which will capture the extremity of an infantile erotic aim beyond the adult categories of possession or submission. But the general term Freud uses is "identification."

IV

When object-love is traced to the primal mother attachment, the distinction between wanting to "have" and "be like" the mother can no longer be maintained: "At the very beginning, in the individual's primitive oral phase, object-cathexis and identification are no doubt indistinguishable from each other."[38] And it is the desire to be identical with, not possess, that seems to describe more closely the infant's primal form of love, as Freud recognized in calling identification "the earliest expression of an emotional tie with another person."[39] Freud describes this earliest tie as that of a "pleasure ego," which approaches the mother as someone to be "absorbed by the ego into itself," "introjected." In the

> [p]reliminary stages of love . . . we recognize the phase of incorporating . . . a type of love which is consistent with *abolishing the object's separate existence*. . . .[40]

Because the primal aim of identification is to overcome the separation of the desired object, Freud continues to refer to its "ambivalence":

> It behaves like a derivative of the first, *oral* phase of the libido, in which the object that we long for and prize is assimilated by eating and is in that way annihilated as such.[41]

But because the pleasure ego immerses the infant in the mother as its own extension, Freud's account cannot help but gesture affirmatively toward infantile love as the (precarious!) achievement of a state of being at one with the mother. For the pleasure ego, relation to the world is "oceanic" rather than antagonistic, "all-embracing" rather than all-exclusive.[42] The constant receptivity of the mother's body to the infant's groping for pleasure sponsors an ego-feeling Freud describes as "limitless narcissism," as if every affection the infant gave to the mother was returned to itself. Indeed, Freud refers to the fully individuated sense of self of a reality ego as only a "shrunken residue" of the self-other unity experienced by the infantile ego.[43]

When Freud speaks in this more affirmative voice about infantile Eros, he allows children the rare privilege of "happy love."[44] Object-love in adults has an element of the zero-sum game about it, an estrangement of libido from self to other which leaves the self impoverished. But because the infant identifies with the mother as that which it is like, it does not distinguish between self-love and object-love. Like the little Narcissus it is, the infant finds and forms the image of its self in the parent as mirror-other.[45] Thus the more a child loves its parents, the more it enriches its own ego:

> The return of the object-libido to the ego and its transformation into narcissism represents, as it were, [the restoration of] happy love once more; and, on the other hand, it is also true that a real happy love corresponds to the primal condition in which object-libido and ego-libido cannot be distinguished.[46]

These narcissistic underpinnings of identification (we love our own image as perceived in the other) are considered in Rieff's account as further evidence of ''[t]he duplicity of erotic sentiment''; all love is partly but a ''devious means of self-love.''[47] But Freud's wide-ranging study of narcissism cannot be reduced to a moralism about human duplicity without also reducing psychoanalysis to a caricature of itself. For example, in his important essay *Mourning and Melancholia,* Freud could be read, I suppose, as exposing the narcissistic motives behind bereavement:

> Reality passes its verdict—that the object no longer exists—upon each single one of the memories and hopes through which the libido was attached to the lost object, and the ego, confronted as it were with the decision whether it will share this fate, is persuaded by the sum of its narcissistic satisfactions in being alive to sever its attachment to the non-existent object.[48]

Yet Freud's point here is hardly that the work of mourning is duplicitous. In laboring in grief to sever libidinal attachment to the dead, the mourner carries out the commands of reality only slowly and gradually, ''bit by bit,'' while ''all the time the existence of the lost object is continued in the mind.''[49] Here the narcissistic return of libido from object to self is at the same time an enlargement of the self through internalization of the other. Narcissism preserves rather than abandons the lost person precisely because the other is too implicated in who the self is to be abandoned without the most painful effort we have ever to make. Ricoeur beautifully expresses this point about the ethical work of mourning:

> Narcissism no longer pursues the every-man-for-himself attitude of the survivor, but the survival of the other in the ego; and so we can say with Freud: ''by taking flight into the ego love escapes extinction.''[50]

What is true of mourning for Freud is true generally of the work of identification, of choosing as love objects persons "like oneself." Identification occupies a singularly important place in psychoanalytic theory because it describes the intersubjective process through which a personality or subject is constituted. "We are bound to suppose that a unity comparable to the ego cannot exist in the individual from the start; the ego has to be developed." [51] Vis-à-vis the parents, the child acquires its first mirror image of who it is, a model or ideal of what it is like. The effect of this first ideal image of an ego is "general and lasting," [52] with the parental image embedding itself as a formative element in the child's emerging identity.

Thus Freud can speak of the earliest stages of ego formation as narcissistic, as the child sees and loves its own image reflected in the parent. But against the common image of narcissism as self-insulation, Freudian narcissism is fundamentally oriented toward the other person as part of one's own identity. The familiar psychology which conceives of the self as absolutely distinct from the other, and which therefore dismisses narcissistic interest in the other as "devious" self-love, is called into question by the concept of identification and the description of an attachment which includes the other in the self there is to be loved. These are complex concepts in Freud, but my point is that Freud's exploration of the narcissistic motives underlying love's identifications speaks to a profound and politically relevant truth about love's work: the closing of space between distinct persons in favor of a self enriched and enlarged by allegiance to the other of such force as to enter into the constitution of an identity. To love the other in whom one sees oneself is, in this sense, to affirm the indispensability of the other to who one is.

Freud did not always carry through with this vision of the essential connectedness of narcissism. When he refers to "primary narcissism," he sometimes has in mind a hypothetical, original mental state, prior to the emergence of an ego, in which libido dwells in the "reservoir" of the id, wholly withdrawn from external reality. [53] Such a state, however, would be the life of a monad, and to affirm it would be to idealize a kind of "back to the womb" movement or the withdrawal from the world characteristic of sleep. [54]

But such a primitive objectless state is hard to fathom, let alone affirm. How indeed would such a monad ever find its libidinal way to the outside world, and to what does narcissism so conceived orient itself in this primitive state prior to ego and object both? As Lacan and others in the French school of psychoanalysis have pointed out, the notion of narcissism would seem to have no meaning prior to the formation of some mirror relation in which the child apprehends for the first time its own reflection.[55] That is to say, there could be no self-image without a sense of the other as well. Perhaps out of appreciation of this point, Freud could not hold fast to his "objectless" description of narcissism. For instance, he distinguishes between an earlier, fragmented stage of autoeroticism, in which sexuality anarchically strives for satisfaction on its own body, and the *later* accomplishment of "narcissism":

> [T]he ego has to be developed. The auto-erotic instincts, however, are there from the very first; so there must be something added to auto-eroticism—a new psychical action—in order to bring about narcissism.[56]

This new psychical action, we have seen, is identification—the formation of a unified, individual personality in place of an earlier anarchy of instincts and pleasures, but also a personality in which one sees not only himself but the parents as well. To seek to return to the "happy love" of narcissism in this sense is thus not to seek return to the womb or withdrawal from the world. It is to love in oneself the image of those other persons whom one is like.

The affirmative work of narcissism and identification is never fully elaborated in psychoanalytic theory. While it is through the desire to be like the other that human beings form ideals and achieve conscience, Freud most often describes this process as one which puts the parent in place of the ego, rather than enriching the ego itself. This is the theme of the Oedipus complex—and of Freud's political psychology in general.

Nonetheless, it is possible to see in the account of identification an augury of more liberating sorts of human attachment. I shall follow that augury here by returning to the infant-parent tie as an example of psychoanalysis' fragile affirmation of Eros beyond the categories of domination and submission.

V

Freud's emphasis on the possessive aim of sexuality cannot encompass the fullness of either the infant's or the mother's pleasure in the act of nursing. For the infant, the pleasure of suckling becomes infused over time with fantasies of incorporation into the mother, of being at one with the mother. For the mother, the emphasis on possessive aims seems lacking, insofar as it reduces the act of nursing to an implausible sequence in which the greedy infant "uses up" the mother.

A more adequate account of suckling as a sexual experience would start by acknowledging that however infants are rigged physically to feel sexual pleasure in the act of suckling for nourishment, a robot holding a bottle would do just as well. But we commonly act on the belief that machine feeding would not do just as well, that babies even when being bottle-fed should be held by human hands. We act, that is to say, on the belief that the mere quenching of hunger does not comprise the whole of the infant's pleasure in nursing, and that in some inexplicable way its sexual pleasure in nursing or bottle feeding is both dependent on the presence of another and heightened by shadowy recognition of the pleasure it gives the "mother" (of whatever gender) even as it takes from her.

In regard to nursing, such interplay of pleasure between child and mother requires a description beyond Freud's anaclitic (possessive) one. The interplay is complex, but we might picture it in the following way. There is an immediate, bodily pleasure to the act of suckling and gaining nourishment whose site is in the infant ("anaclitic sexuality"). But there is also a "second order" pleasure situated in the mother which consists in her coming to take pleasure in knowing that she is the source of the baby's satisfaction. The mother understands that she is "being used" by her baby out of "need." But being used in this way she can affirm as her own pleasure. This use does not draw anything away from her, but, to the contrary, enhances the person she is, creatively enlarges the bounds of her self as her satisfactions become in part some complicated function of her baby's satisfaction.

All of this is to say that the mother can understand the act of nursing, not as being possessed by her infant's needs, but as an experience of being at one with her baby in a way that calls into question both the fixed boundaries between immovable selves and the possibility of assigning a locus in one person rather than the other of the satisfactions going on. The pleasure "of" the nursing mother is the pleasure "in" her baby as well.

But just as the mother takes pleasure in satisfying her baby, one suspects that the infant must somehow (exactly how is a mystery) pick up on and respond to the mother's pleasure. The intercommunication plausibly extends at least so far as this "third order" pleasure back in the infant: the infant's response to the mother's response to the primal physical pleasure in the infant. In this back and forth communication of Eros, the third-order pleasure remains connected to the body, as human Eros this side of neurosis always must remain connected. But the human capacity for communication and reflection has diffused and prolonged the pleasure, and has moved Eros from the original antagonistic and possessive motives for grasping the other to a relation of receptivity to the other's pleasure.

How long the description of this interplay could be coherently carried forward I do not know. But in any such description the location of the pleasure in the child as opposed to the mother would become increasingly problematic as the interplay worked closer to what we would have to regard as a sharing of the same pleasure and as a blurring of the line between mother and child—even though the very fact of interplay would always presuppose and maintain some distinction between them. This blurring of the distinction between infant and mother made possible by the sharing of a common pleasure and happiness is what defines the erotic moment and distinguishes its liberating dependencies and attachments from the hierarchical ones of domination, in which one person is reduced to the status of instrument of the other. However much this erotic moment starts with the physical, its richer dimensions and satisfactions depend on the creative expansion of the self made possible by coming to understand our pleasures as implicated in those of another. These satisfactions can be experienced only in the company of another conceived of, not as antagonist, but as sharer.

This affirmative vision of erotic attachments between infant and parent is fairly suggested by Freud's writings on identification and narcissism. The question for politics, however, is whether the more distant attachments of citizenship can retain a sufficient hold on Eros so as to provide citizens, and not just families, with any meaningful common identity, any sustained sense of being implicated in one another's aspirations. But if Eros can yet empower convictions of citizenship in the modern world, it will not be an Eros taken over intact from childhood and the infant-parent tie. As the opposing force of the death instinct begins to take its toll, the infantile experience of Eros is simply "doomed to extinction."

Death and the Psychology
of Cruelty

"The emotional life of man," Freud remarked, is "made up of
. . . contraries."[1] The preceding analysis focused on the affirmative aspects of the infant-parent tie. But as we have also seen,
Freud insisted that even childhood is ambivalently poised between
love and hate; the desire to be like the parent is pregnant with the
desire to replace the parent.

It is in tracing out this primal conflict between love and hate,
the erotic and the cruel within us, that Freud arrives at his bleak
and tragic vision of psychology and culture. Not self-fulfillment
but self-torment is characteristic of the human condition. There is
in every person an "original, self-subsisting instinctual disposi-
tion" to aggression.[2] Via our loving identification with the other,
we come to control this inclination to cruelty through the institution of remorse and guilt. But this is done only by turning violence
against the self, by internalizing the aggression we wish upon the
other in the form of the self-punishing superego. This dark side of
identification, with its accompanying "sense of guilt," ranks

> as the most important problem in the development of civilization and
> . . . show[s] that the price we pay for our advance in civilization is a loss
> of happiness. . . .[3]

I

Freud came to organize his views about human cruelty under the single concept of a death instinct, or a pure biological urge to come to rest, to throw off the "pain" of organic existence and return to the pure constancy and tension-zero of the "primaeval inorganic state."[4] In this view of human instinctuality, self-destruction is primary and what Freud continues to call "man's natural aggressive instinct" is "the derivative and the main representative of the death instinct." The death instinct itself "eludes our perception"; it operates "silently" when "it is directed inwards" toward dissolution of the organism and comes to light only when "a portion of the instinct is diverted towards the external world . . . as an instinct of aggressiveness and destructiveness." This externalization of destructiveness "constitutes the greatest impediment to civilization."[5]

Prior to proposing a death instinct, Freud had already attended to the centrality of aggression to human nature ("[c]ruelty . . . comes easily to the childish nature," Freud noted in the 1905 edition of *Three Essays on the Theory of Sexuality*), but he treated the aggressive impulse as a component of the sexual instinct, an erotic alloy on the order of sadism and masochism.[6] "[B]eyond any doubt . . . there is an intimate connection between cruelty and the sexual instinct," Freud noted early on, an "aggressive factor in the libido."[7] Such aggression is given shadowy expression in the biting and devouring urges of the oral stage, but its first "organized" form is in the anal activity of "pushing an object out, overcoming it, gaining mastery" (hence Freud's use of the term "sadistic-anal organization"):

> Aggressiveness . . . already shows itself in the nursery almost before property has given up its primal, anal form; it forms the basis of every relation of affection and love among people . . . .[8]

And even after the notion of a death instinct gives these destructive urges an instinctual status independent of sexuality, Freud continues to insist that "we never have to deal with pure life-instincts or death-instincts at all, but only with combinations of them in different degrees."[9] Indeed, Freud reaches the despairing conclusion that only by accomplishing a vast "fusion or coalescence" with the death instinct can Eros accomplish the necessary task of accommodating human destructiveness. He specified three results of this process of instinctual fusion in early childhood: (1) a directing of the death instinct outward toward objects in the external world in the form of aggression, namely the "will to power";[10] through this projection, the death instinct is "pressed into the service of Eros, in that the organism [is] destroying some other thing, whether animate or inanimate, instead of . . . its own self";[11] (2) a binding of part of the instinct to the sexual function in the form of sadism; it is here, "where the death instinct twists the erotic aim in its own sense and yet at the same time fully satisfies the erotic urge, that we succeed in obtaining the clearest insight into its nature and its relation to Eros";[12] (3) a residue of the death instinct left in the organism, which is again bound to Eros as "erotogenic masochism," or sexual pleasure in pain.[13]

Freud's pessimism about erotic life therefore is finally rooted in the deathlike, perverted, or estranged forms Eros assumes in creatures of our sort; the most telltale sign of this perversion of Eros and its alienation away from the desire for union is that there is no separable psychical energy (no analogue to libido) in service to the death instinct. Death manifests itself only by gaining some hold on libido, and once this unholy alliance is forged,

> [i]t really seems as though it is necessary for us to destroy some other thing or person in order not to destroy ourselves, in order to guard against the impulsion to self-destruction. A sad disclosure indeed for the moralist![14]

The tragic consequences of the conflict between Eros and death are sometimes obscured by the conflict *within* erotic life to which Freud also addressed himself. *Civilization and Its Discontents,* Freud's greatest and last statement of his tragic sense of culture will serve as a case in point here. It is not until midway through the book that Freud even broaches the subject of aggression and its contribution to the common unhappiness of the individual in civilization. Up until the midway point, Freud accounts for the malaise haunting civilized life by reference to the tension within erotic life between individual and social interests. The individual seeks the "fully satisfying pleasure" of sexuality, but civilization as a process needs to harness Eros to its own necessities. It thus competes with the individual for the limited pool of psychical energy available, frustrating and then deflecting sexuality into "aim-inhibited" social relationships and activities.[15] The results of this "economic" dispute over the distribution of libido are manifold and painful, and Freud proceeds to highlight them in the essay's first chapters: the taboo on incest and the general tension between family love and wider social attachments; the hostility to sexual freedom and the outlawing of all but reproductive love within monogamous marriage. All of these are serious problems to Freud, fraught with the danger of so suppressing genital sexual activity as to threaten a return of the repressed infantile-incestuous forms of desire and the escape into neurosis.

However problematic they are, Freud is constrained to admit that these sorts of conflicts hardly explain the depth of the unhappiness of cultural man. The dispute between sexuality and sublimation is after all

> a dispute within the economics of the libido [which] does admit of an eventual accommodation . . . however much . . . civilization may oppress the life of the individual to-day.[16]

The search for an explanation of civilization and its discontents thus reaches a dead end when only distributive problems within sexual life are considered. "We are unable to understand what the necessity is which forces civilization into its antagonism to sexuality. There must be some disturbing factor which we have not yet discovered."[17] In search of this disturbing factor, Freud pursues a "clue." Against all that is reasonable to ask of Eros, civilized ethics commands man to "love thy neighbor as thyself"; "love thine enemies." Ethically exaggerated to the point of absurdity, the commandments nonetheless are psychologically revealing:

> The element of truth behind this, which people are so ready to disavow, is that men are not gentle creatures who want to be loved, and who at the most can defend themselves if they are attacked; they are, on the contrary, creatures among whose instinctual endowments is to be reckoned a powerful share of aggressiveness. As a result, their neighbour is for them not only a potential helper or sexual object, but also someone who tempts them to satisfy their aggressiveness on him. . . . *Homo homini lupus.*[18]

Not sexuality alone, then, but

> this inclination to aggression . . . is the factor which disturbs our relations with our neighbour and which forces civilization into such a high expenditure [of energy]. . . . Civilization has to use its utmost efforts in order to set limits to man's aggressive instincts and to hold the manifestations of them in check by . . . the use of methods intended to in-

cite people into identifications and aim-inhibited relationships of love. . . . [19]

In this way, Freud concludes that the absurdity of the Christian commandments regarding love is "justified by the fact that nothing else runs so strongly counter to the original nature of man." [20] And the heart of man's discontent in society, the irreconcilable necessity which causes civilization to suppress, repress, or otherwise deny sexuality in favor of ethically exaggerated affections, is the need to suppress human aggression and send it back where it came from: to the self. It is here that Freud's interpretation of culture becomes tragic, as he traces out in the concluding chapters of *Civilization and Its Discontents* the unholy alliance between Eros and the death instinct in opposition to aggression. Culture depends on the institution of a self-destructive psychology, housed in the superego and played out in the Oedipus complex.

II

The Oedipus complex forms the centerpiece of Freud's analysis of human ambivalence—the "fateful simultaneous conjunction of love for the one parent and hatred of the other as a rival." [21] Freud considered the formation of such a complex to be universal and its passing to comprise the crucial renunciations upon which morality and culture depend.

The seeds of an Oedipus complex are sown in early infancy. As we have seen, a child forms two kinds of erotic ties: an identification with the parent (typically the father) as an ego ideal or model, on the one hand, and an incestuous sexual object-choice (typically of the mother), on the other. The two forms of relation "subsist side by side for a time without any mutual influence or interference. In consequence of the irresistible advance toward a unification of mental life, they come together at last; and the normal Oedipus complex originates from their confluence." [22] The incestuous object-choice of one parent becomes an act of rivalry against the other and forces the preexisting identification (which we have seen is ambivalent from the beginning) into an aggravated, hostile pattern. However, "the hatred of the parent, so provoked, is unable to gain uninhibited sway . . . over the mind; it has to contend against [the] old-established affection and admiration for the very same person," as well as against fantasies of punishment and castration from the more powerful figure.

What Freud considered to be the normal resolution of the complex was the surrender of the sexual object-relation with the parent and the resolution of the parental identification in favor of its affectionate rather than aggressive dimension. What gives this sexual renunciation its ethical and social content, as well as its pathos, is that the child internalizes the parental image with which it identifies as its own ideal, indeed takes over the parental ideal as its own conscience or superego.

But against the narcissistic dimension of identification discussed in Chapter Two, the Oedipal culmination of identification has a violence about it, an inexplicably severe and self-punishing aspect. The parental image internalized as the superego watches over the ego "like a garrison in a conquered city." [23] It confronts the host ego with a "harshly restraining, cruelly prohibiting quality" that we call "ordinary normal morality." [24]

Why should the superego be so sinister? The straightforward explanation is that it merely replicates internally the punishing and authoritative work of the parent on the outside. [25] But this view of the superego as undistorting mirror of the actual parent is contradicted by the clinical evidence:

> the superego seems to have made a one-sided choice and to have picked out only the parents' strictness and severity, their prohibiting and punitive function, whereas their loving care seems not to have been taken over. . . . If the parents have really enforced their authority with severity we can easily understand the child's in turn developing a severe superego. But contrary to our expectation, experience shows that the superego can acquire the same characteristics of relentless severity even if the upbringing had been mild. . . . [26]

> Experience shows, however, that the severity of the superego which a child develops in no way corresponds to the severity of treatment which he has himself met with. The severity of the former seems to be independent of that of the latter. A child who has been very leniently brought up can acquire a very strict conscience. [27]

Freud therefore suggested that the theory of the superego would fit the facts better if the straightforward explanation were stood on its head: instead of the cruelty of conscience representing the father punishing the child's aggressive desires, conscience seems more accurately to be the child's own but disguised aggression attempting to punish the father. The child takes the father "into" himself, identifies with him—and then treats him with all the aggression he stifled in his external behavior:

> By means of identification he takes the unattackable authority into himself. The authority now turns into his superego and enters into possession of all the aggressiveness which a child would have liked to exercise against it. The child's ego has to content itself with the unhappy role of the authority—the father—who has thus been degraded. Here, as so often, the [real] situation is reversed. "If I were the father and you were the child, I should treat you badly." [28]

The significance of thus standing the superego on its head is not to be missed. For what Freud is saying, in effect, is that our morality *is* our aggressiveness. Conscience "does not so much . . . represent the severity which one has experienced from [the parent] or which one attributes to [him]; it represents rather one's own aggressiveness towards it." [29] The superego is a reservoir for "one's own aggressive energy which has not been used and which one now directs against that inhibiting authority." [30]

In this way, the inexplicable sense of guilt plaguing the individual comes to explain itself. The sense of guilt is a way of tormenting the father through tormenting oneself. It is an act of masochism that expresses an act of sadism. [31] No wonder, then, that humanity seems fated to dwell in guilt. For even when one renounces hostile wishes toward the father and becomes a moral person, morality itself, ironically, continues to express the same hostility:

> What happens . . . to render his desire for aggression innocuous? Something very remarkable, which we should never have guessed and which is nevertheless quite obvious. His aggressiveness is introjected, internalized; it is, in point of fact, sent back to where it came from—that is, it is directed toward his own ego. There it is taken over by a portion of the ego . . . as superego, and which now, in the form of "conscience," is ready to put into action against the ego the same harsh aggressiveness that the ego would have liked to satisfy upon other[s]. . . . The tension between the harsh superego and the ego . . . is called by us the sense of guilt; it expresses itself as a need for punishment. [32]

Nowhere are Freud's criticisms of superego morality expressed more poignantly than in *The Ego and the Id,* the very book which officially introduced the superego into the topography of the soul. Common sense has it that the human capacity to form ideals is also the capacity "for the suppression of aggressiveness. The fact remains, however, as we have stated it: the more a man controls his aggressiveness, the more intense becomes his ideal's inclination to aggressiveness against his ego. It is like a displacement, a turning round upon his own ego." [33] Freud therefore concludes that the phenomenon of idealization is a violent one, with the self the victim of its own ideals, of its own untransformed aggressions.

All of this, to say the least, is surprising. One might expect that renunciation of outward aggression would lead to good conscience, to a superego watching over its charge less suspiciously. But "the actual state of things seems to be a reversal of this." [34] The more one refrains from expressing aggression toward others, the more "this backward-flowing part of the instinct of destruction comes to expression . . . as an intensified masochism [and] the more strict and sensitive . . . conscience becomes." [35]

Since the superego has its origin in human aggression internalized, Freud despondently concludes that "[w]hat is now holding sway in the superego is, as it were, a pure culture of the death instinct. . . ." [36] As Ricoeur expresses Freud's point,

> Caught between a murderous id and a tyrannical and punishing conscience, the ego appears to have no recourse other than self-torment or the torturing of others by diverting its aggressiveness toward them. [37]

Not the least of reasons for placing superego morality on the side of the death instinct is its insatiable press for self-punishment. As we have seen, the child is unable to obtain the full benefit of its surrender to parental authority; the feared, external punishment is replaced by the punitive sense of guilt as the superego picks up on the internal survival of the child's rebellious erotic desires:

> This constitutes a great economic disadvantage in the erection of a superego. . . . Instinctual renunciation now no longer has a completely liberating effect. . . . A threatened external unhappiness—loss of love and punishment on the part of the external authority—has been exchanged for a permanent internal unhappiness, for the tension of the sense of guilt. [38]

III

Freud's Oedipal categories are remarkably sex specific. With rare exceptions he insisted that the authoritative presence in childhood is always the father and that the superego takes over the father as the child's own ideal. Although Freud might have defended this equation of father and authority by referring to prevailing social structures, he chose an alternative explanation, as is well known. What disqualifies the mother from serving as a model for her children (boys and girls alike) is the perception of her body as castrated and therefore powerless.

For a boy, this perception fuels fantasies that the father-rival will punish him also with castration were the father to sense the son's sexual designs on the mother. This fear causes the boy to surrender his object-love for the mother, as well as to exaggerate the identification of his father as his ideal. Girls

> develop an Oedipus-complex, too, a super-ego and a latency period. May one ascribe to it also a phallic organization and a castration complex? The answer is in the affirmative, but it cannot be the same as in the boy. The feministic demand for equal rights between the sexes does not carry far here; the morphological difference must express itself in differences in the development of the mind. "Anatomy is Destiny," to vary a saying of Napoleon's. The little girl's clitoris behaves at first just like a penis, but by comparing herself with a boy playfellow the child perceives that she has "come off short," and takes this fact as ill-treatment and as a reason for feeling inferior.[39]

With this feeling of inferiority, the girl turns away from her mother, blames her for her loss, and turns to the father in hopes of compensation:

> The girl passes over—by way of symbolic analogy, one may say—from the penis to a child; her Oedipus-complex culminates in the desire, which is long cherished, to be given a child by her father as a present, to bear him a child.[40]

It is clear that this theory assigns to female psychology a status little better than a pathology. Women are doomed to feelings of inferiority and the outcome of their Oedipus complex will always have far less social significance then the Oedipus complex in boys. In boys, castration dread leads them to renounce decisively the search for sexual satisfaction in the family; they are propelled out into the larger community in search of new satisfactions as fathers themselves. For girls, castration dread solidifies their Oedipal attachment to the father, wedding them to the compensation of femininity, which is supposedly having babies. Thus Freud could say that the Oedipus complex never quite passes in women, never quite gets free of father-love.[41]

Freud's scientific side misled him into believing that his views on the female Oedipus complex were supported by clinical observations of so-called "penis envy" in girls. But penis envy is a term of interpretation, not observation. And there would seem very little illumination in the claims that women are condemned by biology to understand themselves as inferior, that little girls can interpret their lack of a penis only as a defect. Even assuming for argument that such a self-understanding has traditionally accompanied female development, psychoanalysis itself is the stage of human consciousness which destroys the hold of this interpretation on female (and male) minds. Psychoanalysis points out, after all, that the source of such feelings of inferiority is in a mistake that can succumb to education and to the truth that women are not castrated.

How great is the damage to psychoanalysis as a whole which stems from Freud's own pejorative views on women? On the one hand, it is not easy to compartmentalize Freud's writings on female sexuality; they form a central part of his theory of moral development in children. On the other hand, psychoanalysis is yet capable of a more affirmative understanding of feminism. As the work of Dinnerstein and others has shown, this more affirmative teaching stems from Freud's late writings and the importance he assigned there to the pre-Oedipal attachment to the mother.[42] Here Freud, against his own Oedipal categories, appreciated that the mother was the central—indeed typically the only—adult presence in her child's early life. No longer a castrated male, the mother represented the nourishing body in which the child found its pleasure and its initial understanding of the world as joyous. Child psychology then became a process of weaning and separating the child from the mother's body, a separation that replaced the "oceanic" experience of the world as receptive to one's pleasure with an "Oedipal" experience of the world as mired in conflict, rivalry, violence, and aggression.

These later writings of Freud cannot avoid calling into question the cultural dominance of male-oriented Oedipal psychology. They point, in continuity with Freud's other writings, to the troubling and surprising connection between the Oedipal superego and human aggression. These writings also point to the loss of an earlier, more benign ethic of receptivity that centered on the idealized image of the mother. A revision of Freud's theories in light of his belated discovery of pre-Oedipal psychology would thus seem a necessary task for psychoanalysis in the future.

IV

In his clinical studies, Freud gave particular attention to the metamorphosis of Oedipal aggression into conscientious but self-repressive obedience to the father.

There is, for instance, the mystery presented by Little Hans, who shortly before his fifth birthday developed an acute fear of horses. The predominant element in the fear was that a horse would bite him were he to venture on the street or that, conversely, a horse itself might be hurt, by falling down under the heavy load of the cart it pulled. To Hans' father, this phobia of horses being hurt or hurting seemed all the more strange in light of Hans' prior joy in "playing" at horses with other children or "riding" his father the horse.[43]

But the prior source of pleasure "turned into an object of fear," and the task of the analysis (conducted in person by the father, in consultation with Freud) was to decipher what, if anything, Hans expressed obliquely in his "horse nonsense." Was there anything about his attitude toward the persons around him that fueled and found symbolic representation in the language of horses, which, after all, did sometimes literally fall down or bite?

As the conversations proceeded between Hans and his father, Hans' prior associations between horses and penises were made apparent. For the previous year and a half, Hans' father had been aware of his son's "lively interest" in his own "widdler" and his curiosity about female genitals. When observation of his seven-day-old sister showed no widdler, Hans retreated into the remark, "her widdler's still quite small . . . [W]hen she grows up it'll get bigger all right." Hans took his curiosity to his mother, who assured him that she did have a widdler, to which her son replied, "I thought you were so big you'd have a widdler like a horse."[44]

Hans' interest in his widdler was practical as well as theoretical and led to the conventional demand from his mother that he stop masturbating or "I shall send for Dr. A to cut off your widdler." Coupled with his unsatisfactory search for the female genital, this idea of being separated from his penis had its Oedipal effect on the child's fantasy life. The horse as father (big; big widdler; the father had been Hans' play horse) would indeed bite Hans, would indeed castrate him were the father to know of the son's sexual desire for the mother and the corollary of hate for the father. This the child sought to avoid by staying indoors and away from the horse punishment. But Hans' submission to fear was more than a matter of developing a passing phobia. What one witnesses in his case is conscience in the making, the moral transformation of his desires from Oedipal aggression against horses to fear of horses to fear for horses' safety. In moving through these steps, Hans accomplishes the normally submissive resolution of Oedipal hostility. The horse phobia was simply one of many appropriate ways in which this complex of hidden desires toward the father could find symbolic expression.

Freud thought it perfectly normal for children to have such Oedipal phobias. They were a kind of rite of passage. But some persons—neurotics—never satisfactorily resolve their Oedipal ambivalence; even as adults they remain fixated in guilt on their aggressive-hostile feelings toward the parent and seek to punish themselves in their love and work. From the time of puberty onward,

> the human individual has to devote himself to the great task of detaching himself from his parents, and not until that task is achieved can he cease to be a child and become a member of the social community. . . . By neurotics, however, no [detachment] at all is arrived at: the son remains all his life bowed beneath his father's authority and he is unable to transfer his libido to an outside sexual object. With the relationship changed round, the same fate can await the daughter. In this sense the Oedipus complex may justly be regarded as the nucleus of the neuroses.[45]

Prime among such adult Oedipuses is Freud's patient known as the Rat Man.[46] As a young man in the army, the Rat Man heard a story about rats boring into the anuses of prisoners as a punishment-torture. He responded to the story with increasingly obsessive frenzy that such a punishment threatened his father, even though his father had died previously, and his own ladyfriend, whom he dared not marry on account of the opposition his father had expressed prior to his death. Freud finds, in the Rat Man's inability to make an independent choice of love object and in his moralistic obsessions over his father's safety, the lingering results of an Oedipal hostility of more than the average intensity. In the Rat Man's childhood, early sexual experiences and the severity of the father's actual punishments combined to provoke the child's aggressive hostility to a marked degree. The passage through the Oedipus complex thus required heightened repression of that hostility or indeed of any resistance to the father colored by hostility. In this way, the early provocation of aggression called forth its cowardly opposite, a personality unable to make choices in life (marriage) in opposition to the father's wish and reacting to accidental adult experiences (the Rat story) by supermoral defense against the latent hostility to which such experiences spoke. The Rat Man's moral will was so totally controlled by guilt that even after his father died he remained unable to marry against the father's desires and he fell ill of the continuing plague of bad conscience.

Freud's treatment of the Rat Man is especially interesting, in light of the Rat Man's insistence that his relation to his father had been of the warmest and most intimate sort. Freud does not challenge the reality of this self-understanding. After all, it is "precisely such intense love . . . that [is] the condition of the repressed hatred." [47] What psychoanalysis *is* interested in exposing is the partiality of the understanding that sees children as uncomplicated in their affections. In the Rat Man's case, love for the father can shed *some* light on his difficulties with his ladyfriend and on his fear for his father's safety. But when obsession with his father's safety continues even after his father's death and when it takes the incredible form of fear that his father may fall victim to the Rat punishment, then Freud insists we must seek the further illumination that comes from confronting our own darkest projects and the extent to which even (especially) our deepest loves are compromised by an element of hate and aggression.

Both the Rat Man and Little Hans could be classified as "obsessive neurotics." In the separate neurosis of melancholic depression, Freud accomplishes his most brilliant unmasking of the inauthentic functioning of superego morality. The defining aspect of this kind of depression is the periodic loss of one's normal sense of self-worth. Freud describes the condition as one in which the superego attacks the ego, "becomes over-severe, abuses the poor ego, humiliates it and ill-treats it, threatens it with [dire] punishments. . . ." [48] What is this all about? What has the person done to deserve punishment?

Freud's answer is suggested in his root comparison of melancholia with the work of mourning. As discussed in Chapter Two, mourning is the process by which libido, in obedience to the reality principle, begins the gradual process of withdrawing its attachments to the dead. During the course of grief, the ego is totally but painfully absorbed in its work and indifferent to the external world. The indifference, however, is temporary, and the absorption of the mourner in grief is successful to the extent it finally detaches libido from the dead and returns it to the living.

Melancholia is likewise a case of mourning the loss of a loved person through death or desertion. However, in melancholia the withdrawal of libido is accompanied by the sudden decline in self-respect. The mournful ego becomes morosely involved in self-criticism through a process Freud seeks to explain as follows. Like the mourner, the melancholic resists reality and seeks to preserve the lost person by identifying his own ego with that of the other. But he does so in a highly negative and critical fashion. Always ambivalent to begin with, a love relation lost sets hate free to take its revenge on the ego, now identified with the other. But of course this is an act of revenge that is at the same time punishment of oneself for harboring such vengeance. The loss of self-regard characteristic of melancholia is an act of moral masochism hiding an act of sadism; the depression owes its overseverity to its function as unconscious punishment and perpetual atonement for harboring impulses inconsistent with one's ideals.

Alongside Little Hans, the Rat Man, and melancholics, Freud's portrait of Dostoyevsky may serve as a final example of the self-destructiveness of guilty conscience. Despite great admiration for the Russian novelist, Freud offers the criticism that the religiously orthodox Dostoyevsky made himself one politically with humanity's jailers. "The future of human civilization will have little to thank him for." [49] This condemnation stems from Dostoyevsky's inability to come to terms with his own father complex. Dostoyevsky wrote to a friend that he was plagued by a guilt whose source remained unknown to him. "[H]e seemed to himself a criminal and could not get rid of the feeling that . . . he had committed some great misdeed, which oppressed him." [50]

What was Dostoyevsky's great misdeed? In childhood, Freud finds the novelist already engaged in the self-punishment of deathlike or epileptic seizures, which can be understood as a father-identification on the part of his ego, permitted by his superego as a punishment. "You wanted to kill your father in order to be your father yourself. Now you *are* your father, but a dead father."[51]

In Freud's view, Dostoyevsky never freed himself from his early filial guilt. The penitence he showed in his writings and in his personal life, the moral attitude of "complete submission" to the authority of Church and Czar, were for his ego but "masochistic satisfaction," for his superego but "punishment satisfaction," a more intellectual discharge of the same needs accomplished in childhood through his pseudo-epilepsy.

Freud realizes that it may appear as if he has offered a moral judgment on the worth of Dostoyevsky's ideas. He does not mean to do so, he hastens to add, content to let the chips fall where they may after exposing the "intellectual inhibition" of filial guilt that kept Dostoyevsky from reaching conscious or rational decisions on matters involving religion and the state.

V

The resemblance between Freud's derivation of the superego and Nietzsche's genealogy of morals was noted in Freud's own lifetime. Nietzsche relentlessly took to task the Kantian notion of objective moral judgments made in reference to some category of right or duty; behind such an objective ethic was only the subjective will to power of those too impotent to count in a world which valued self-affirmation.[52] The Kantian concept of duty was nothing more then the suppressed aggression of the weak returning in its most virulent form—"spiritual vengeance," the festering, underground hatred of the weak for the strong. Nietzsche prepared to welcome the return of the repressed will to power with open arms.

Late in his life, Freud struck up a correspondence with a young German writer at work on an essay comparing Freud to Nietzsche. The author wrote to Freud that

> [t]o me it seems that you have achieved everything that Nietzsche intuitively felt to be his task, without his being really able to achieve it. . . .
> He longed for a world beyond Good and Evil; by means of analysis you have discovered a world to which the phrase actually applies. Analysis has reversed all values; it has conquered Christianity, disclosed the true Anti-Christ, and liberated the spirit of resurgent life from the ascetic ideal.[53]

Although Freud does share with Nietzsche a criticism of the conventional morality of guilt as a masked expression of human aggression and as a destruction of the vitality of Eros, Freud hardly yearned for Nietzsche's will to power or for "resurgent life," instinctual liberation, or any other ethic of spontaneity. Freud is ultimately a defender of moral authority, but the power and scope of his critique of the superego often obscures his position and makes psychoanalysis *seem* as if it too might yearn for a world liberated from good and evil:

> We can present society with a blunt calculation that what is described as its morality calls for a bigger sacrifice than it is worth and that its proceedings are not based on honesty and do not display wisdom.[54]

But at times Freud makes clear that his moral criticism has a more focused target in the reigning Kantian system of morality as duty. Freud singles out Kant's categorical imperative as the philosophical cousin to the psychoanalytic superego, calling each "cruel" and a "direct inheritance from the Oedipus complex."[55] Freud never went on to elaborate on the cruelty of the Kantian imperative, but much of the significance of psychoanalysis for questions of liberation lies in its implicit anti-Kantianism. For Kant, moral duty finds its justification wholly apart from the consequences it has for human happiness. It is true, Kant acknowledges, that all men by nature aim at achieving happiness. But the desire for happiness nonetheless cannot form an objective basis for moral judgment because persons disagree on what their happiness consists in. There is no one conception that persons can be asked to obey without surrendering the freedom of their will to conceive of another.[56]

Thus if obedience to moral law is to fit with human freedom, it must find its justification wholly apart from what human beings happen to want. It must, in Kant's awesomely anti-Freudian phrase, "proudly reject all kinship with the inclinations."[57] Kant went on to locate such a moral faculty in the autonomous will of human beings, the ability of human beings to transcend the world of senses and desire and to participate in a process of deliberation unconditioned by particular kinds of aims and purposes. This process of deliberation puts aside the question of what will make men and women happy. It seeks to comprehend only what it is categorically right to do, regardless of consequences. That we have this capacity to will to do what is right, and not merely what is good for us, demonstrates our freedom of will. That we choose to do our duty, even at the cost of happiness, shows our morality.

Since what makes a given course of behavior "right" is wholly apart from its consequences for human happiness, moral duty for Kant is unconditional and allows no exceptions in the mere name of what, it turns out, makes men happy in a given time or space. Kant himself offered no illusions about the sternness of the ethic he endorsed. Most persons, he conceded,

> discover that they have in fact only brought more trouble on their heads than they have gained in the way of happiness. On this account they come to envy, rather than despise, the more common run of men, who are closer to the guidance of mere natural instinct.[58]

In *Civilization and Its Discontents,* Freud restates Kant's own sense of the unhappy dimension to moral duty. But Freud's statement calls into question the distinction between desire and duty upon which the Kantian obligation to do one's duty even at the cost of happiness depends. The content of the categorical imperative is just another, albeit quite primal, desire: the desire to be like the parent. Worse, this desire is fused with an urge to aggression internalized.

It is commonly argued that accounts of the psychological origins of moral judgment, however complete, cannot dispose of the further question of whether those judgments (whatever their origin) are supportable on rational grounds. But surely this familiar motive/ground distinction cannot avail against Freud's genealogy of conscience, as at least some moral philosophers have recognized.[59] For to apprehend with Freud the *origins* of conscience is to apprehend the *persistence* over time of the work of the death instinct within conscience. Moral duty always remains within the natural history of desire—it has no "higher" source—and it is a history which, in its superego stage, tensely shuttles between aggression and self-destruction.

Civilization and Its Discontents ends on a note of resignation about this death face of conscience and culture. It is to be hoped that the tendency of Eros to hold persons together will overcome the countertrend toward destruction and dissolution of life. But the hope is precarious, the moral use of death to check aggression through guilt a perpetual danger:

[M]ay we not be justified in reaching the diagnosis that, under the influence of cultural urges, some civilizations, or some epochs of civilization—possibly the whole of mankind—have become neurotic?[60]

Always the honest broker, Freud leaves this question unanswered. But for the physician even to contemplate extending his diagnosis from the individual to the social level is to betray awareness that psychoanalysis ultimately cannot leave unchallenged the ordinary "cruel" ethic, the "common unhappiness" to which it returns even liberated individuals.

Chapter Four

Eros, Death, and Politics

The preceding analysis traced the work of Eros and death in the process Freud calls "identification"—the basic form of human relation which binds a family, internalizes authority, and sponsors civilization. The concept of identification is, I have argued, a suggestive gesture toward the ideal of union between self and other beyond domination and submission. At the same time, Freud makes clear that the civil state depends on a more sinister, Oedipal form of identification among creatures so naturally destructive.

Freud's teachings about politics are a skillful elaboration of the ambivalent love-hate relation to authority contained within the Oedipus complex. He appreciated that, for better or worse, politics is about the closing of distance between persons, the transformative allegiance to a common life that goes beyond the instrumental ties of self-interested actors left unchanged by their social circumstance. Precisely because of this threat to human distance and individuation, it is fair to say that Freud himself mistrusted politics only slightly less than religion. Nevertheless, his affirmative contribution to political psychology is to expose the superficiality of the conventional view of political community as no more than the networking of self-interest. Love and work are the parents of civilization, Freud noted. Therefore one could imagine, in tune with the popular view,

> a cultural community consisting of double individuals [i.e., couples] who, libidinally satisfied in themselves, are connected with one another through the bonds of common work and common interests.[1]

But, Freud continues,

> this desirable state of things does not, and never did, exist. Reality shows . . . civilization is not content with the ties we have so far allowed it. It aims at binding the members of the community together in a libidinal way as well and employs every means to that end. It favours every path by which strong identifications can be established between the members of the community, and it summons up aim-inhibited libido on the largest scale so as to strengthen the communal bond by relations of friendship.[2]

Of course, few if any political philosophers have ever taught that overlapping self-interest (what Freud refers to above as common work and common interests) is sufficient in itself to constitute a political community. Even social contract theorists such as Hobbes, who have rested the legitimacy of government on its service to a rational calculus of self-interest, have also demanded an act of obligation—a promise or contract—which binds the person *in foro interno* (in the inner forum). But the solidity of a contract community is still that between selves whose interests are fixed outside of and prior to the contract. The attachments formed, however irreversible, are thus distant, a matter of finding one another's company attractive at best, unavoidable at worst, on the way to precalculated and separate ends.

Via the concept of identification, Freud restores to the political arena the formation of deeper attachments and allegiances that call into question the rooted boundaries between selves. Political community is founded *more* by love than work, more by Eros than economics: "[S]ocial feeling is based upon the *reversal* of what was first a hostile feeling into a positively-toned tie in the nature of an *identification*"[3] (emphasis added). But Freud's views on the erotic drama of political identification are halting; at least on the surface, psychoanalysis takes its stand with those who have long seen in love the most antipolitical of passions. For, as we saw in Chapter One, when politics is practiced as if it were love, it destroys the difference between public and private. It brings love out into the light and distorts it through publicity and loss of intimacy—Freud's case against the "small modicum" of feeling that could possibly characterize the Christian love of every man.[4] Meanwhile, politics itself descends into the dark and as a false and furtive lover insinuates itself into intimacies that have no relevance for public life.

To appreciate Freud's despair about political life, therefore, is to see that politics goes badly for him not just because human beings are so inclined to cruel aggressions but because they are so much in need of the consolation of love. "[C]onsolation . . . at bottom that is what they are all demanding—the wildest revolutionaries no less passionately than the most virtuous believers."[5] Politics, on this view, is just another part of man's universal neurosis, "cunning devices adopted by man the infant against being left alone,"[6] against the perpetual anxiety that flows from infantile conflict between the desire to be loved, on the one hand, and the hostilities engendered by pursuit of instinctual gratification on the other.

I

If individual neuroses can be understood fully only by reference to the childhood trauma they reenact, then the study of why politics goes so poorly must also be a study of origins for Freud. Throughout his career, he searched for those origins, reading widely in anthropology and in Darwinism, and speculating often about deep, dark occurrences in prehistory whose memory constitutes "an archaic heritage" for every newborn child.[7] In putting forth these speculations, Freud found ready-made for his use the imagery of a "state of nature" and a "social contract." But his use of this imagery is to radically different effect than its classical use in Hobbes or Locke. Freud puts forward his Oedipalized version of the state of nature a full four times in his writings, but the story is basically along the following lines.

One can imagine a human animal bereft of any inner need to associate with others of his species except in the most fleeting and periodic of manners. But long, long ago, the human animal evolved into a being whose sexual urge was permanent, not periodic; from and after that development in the species, men and women have been "horde animals" even within the state of nature.[8]

But what made this first horde form of association possible was

not perception of some common interest or mutual benefit in
group life; its basis was brute domination by one male of the
women he desired and the children they produced. According to
Freud, the man would have wanted to monopolize and control the
sources of his sexual pleasure and the women would have wanted
not to be separated from their offspring.[9] By protecting the women
and the offspring, therefore, male domination found its justification, kept the peace, provided security, and must have seemed
even necessary.

In Freud's version, the revolutionary potential within such an
act of domination is not between father and mother (although
matriarchy does briefly follow the father's overthrow[10]), but between father and son. Whatever kind of affection could have
developed within conditions of domination, hatred for the father's
tyranny and monopoly of sexual pleasure must have been great.
This hatred, Freud speculates, led many times over to sons banding
together to slay the father and even to devour him, being the can-
nibals they were.[11] But however much they hated the father tyrant,
they also identified with him and admired him as their protector.
Ambivalence greeted their revolutionary deed, therefore, and led
the brothers into feelings of remorse and guilt. From such remorse
came the twin acts of atonement that mark for Freud the passage
from family to wider society. On the one hand, the brothers raised
their murdered father as their living god, stronger than he had ever
been; on the other hand, they renounced the sexual satisfactions
which had motivated the rebellion, introducing in place of instinctual license the first great piece of shared or collective renunciation—the incest taboo. Freud dates from the incest taboo the
emergence of a new principle of social organization; a

> sort of social contract . . . came about with a *renunciation of instinct*, a
> recognition of mutual *obligations*, the introduction of definite *institu-
> tions*, pronounced inviolable (holy)—that is to say, the beginnings of
> morality and justice. Each individual renounced his ideal of acquiring
> his father's position for himself and of possessing his mothers and
> sisters.[12]

However, what makes the principle of a contract community
"new" is not the sheer fact of instinctual suppression—the father
had demanded that of his sons with a vengeance. The new element
is that this suppression can be in the interests of all rather than the
one, can be self-imposed rather than externally coerced. Freud

speaks the language of the social contract, but what he gestures toward, as opposed to Hobbes and Locke but similar to Rousseau, is a complex psychological and moral transformation in the nature of human desire as social replaces natural man. Indeed, Freud is led to a conclusion about the social contract similar to the conclusions he had offered about the superego: it institutionalizes the taboo on incest through *self*-repression with an efficiency at least the equal of the father's domination. And whereas repression serving only the father's continued domination could be regarded as unnecessary to civilization, the ethically transforming self-repressions enshrined in the contract seem the price we must pay for associating in peace on some basis other than the father's domination. In Marcuse's term, the brother clan turns out simply to be "ever 'better' domination."[13] Father murderers turn into father worshippers in an act of unconscious guilt for their misdeed. Eros, which liberated had aligned itself with the most horrible of aggressions, is now permanently reined in by the incest taboo abroad and the superego within. This is why Freud can conclude that the brother clan is bound to be always a precarious moment in human history, preparing the way internally for surrender in guilt to new father figures. The brothers come to prefer their previous postures as sons, children, and dependents, and patriarchal organization of the family and of culture in general returns.

According to Freud, these primitive Oedipal deeds of our ancestors have in some shadowy way come to form a "collective content" in the individual unconscious, "a memory trace" in the infantile id of the experiences of former generations.[14] Thus individual psychology is doubly Oedipalized: the fantasies that accompany the child-parent conflict spin out an Oedipal history of their own; but there is, according to Freud, also a phylogenetically inherited guilt, an unconscious which is what it is because the history of the species has been as it has. At times, Freud defended this notion of phylogenetic inheritance only haltingly.[15] Other times, he held out his anthropology as empirically valid.[16] But the reasons Freud was tempted into buttressing his account of individual Oedipal psychology with a mythic account of the species' prehistory are obscure. The difficulties with that kind of buttressing are, after all, enormous. First, Freud can hardly treat the primal crime as capable of empirical verification, since, by definition, he is hypothesizing a prehistory no longer available to knowledge. Second, even if we allow the probability that Oedipal-type crimes occurred in prehistory, Freud can make the required connection between those events and the contemporary individual unconscious only by arguing, à la Lamarck, that the remorse acquired by our ancestors over their deeds was so "important" and/or "repeated" that it proved capable of inheritance.[17] Not only is this view of inheritance of memories and acquired characteristics rejected by the science of genetics; Freud leaves wholly unspecified what he means by "important" and "repeated." Coronations of monarchs and seventh games of World Series are also important and frequent events. In Freud's theory there is no way to explain why memories of such events do not also prove capable of phylogenetic transmission.

It may be that Freud was struggling in his phylogenesis to avoid postulating a fixed human nature, formed outside of and antecedent to the evolutionary history of the species. Marcuse, for one, understands Freud's historical speculations as serving such a purpose, at least as symbolic summary of the history of domination and repression and the way in which such history can "sink down" to the level of human instinctuality.[18] But it is difficult to see why Freud needed to postulate mythological prehistory in order to express the historicity of human nature. Psychoanalysis already accomplishes that expression, by tracing the history of a life from infancy to adulthood. To be sure, psychoanalysis also insists on there being a structure to human development that is more than the sum of our individual conditionings. But when the nature of our being includes a force as formative as infantile sexuality, then Freud has already made the case for studying psychology from the developmental, historical point of view. Freud's use of phylogenesis to reinforce the truth of the Oedipal categories of development seems gratuitous. His shrewdness about politics and submission can rest comfortably on the historical cycle of rebellion and remorse embedded in family life. In relation to this cycle, fear of loss of love stands out as the Achilles heel of human psychology, a vulnerability that leads us to approach political society as if it were the family writ large.

II

Freud entertained a great fear regarding the conditions of modern political life and what new forms the domination symbolized in the myth of the primal horde was likely to assume. On the individual level, we know that neurotics reenact infantile conflicts until the heart of the matter is subjected to rational reflection and resolution. On the political level, the species seems similarly fated to dwell in the cycle of rebellion against and submission to patriarchal rule until the sources of our shared Oedipal drama are comprehended and dissolved.

An exile from Hitler's *Auschland*, Freud was occupied in his last years with the barbarism which human instinct armed to the teeth might yet accomplish. And he closes *Civilization and Its Discontents* with an almost prayerful hope that Eros might yet find a way to accomplish the unity of mankind it intends. Nothing less powerful than Eros as a political tie will do; in the end people either love or hate, and in a final line added to *Civilization and Its Discontents* in 1939, Freud resigns himself to science's inability to predict or assume the survival of the species.[19]

But if a politics of love is necessary to stave off the politics of cruelty, there are nonetheless grave dangers in the solution. In *Group Psychology and the Analysis of the Ego,* Freud puts forward what on the surface is supposed to be a neutral account of Eros as the indispensable force behind every cohesive group. But a critical voice keeps surfacing in the description of erotic political mechanics, as Freud traces out the debased love people in groups can share—and the obedience beyond conscience it portends. The achievement of love in private, we have seen, is the creation of ethical constraint as the child takes over the parent as its ideal. The achievement is qualified by its compromise with the death instinct, but it forms the basis of the only culture we know. The further "ethical" achievement of politics threatens to abolish the individuated superego in favor of the group itself as moral authority.

Freud's analysis in *Group Psychology* is locked into an almost single-minded attention to the "extreme passion for authority," the "thirst for obedience" which seems to color social relations. The political philosopher's question about authority—is it legitimate?—does not concern Freud directly, and what he dwells upon are the psychological effects of life within authoritatively structured relations, whether legitimate or not. In this regard, it is a fact to remark upon that persons in cohesive groups (from the camaraderie of the school dormitory to the rank orderings of the army) behave at times as if under hypnosis; they suffer a marked decline in their critical-reasoning capacities and in their feelings of individuation. So often they are caught up in the contagion of easy emotion and suggestions: what the group does or the leader orders,

I shall do. Freud quotes approvingly this statement of the nine-teenth-century psychologist LeBon:

> We see, then, that the disappearance of the conscious personality, the predominance of the unconscious personality, the turning by means of suggestion and contagion of feelings and ideas in an identical direc-tion . . . these, we see, are the principal characteristics of the in-dividual forming part of a group. He is no longer himself, but has become an automaton who has ceased to be guided by his will.[20]

Freud's own description of group life is equally pejorative and sur-prisingly one-sided. The intensity of the group tie is accomplished by "the lack of independence and initiative in their members, the similarity in the reactions of all of them, their reduction, so to speak, to the level of group individuals."[21] The criticism goes on: "[the] weakness of intellectual ability, the lack of emotional restraint, the incapacity for moderation and delay, the inclination to exceed every limit in the expression of emotion and to work it off completely in the form of action . . . show an unmistakable pic-ture of a regression of mental activity to an earlier stage such as we are not surprised to find among savages or children."[22] Perhaps, Freud hastened to add, such regression could be avoided in highly organized or "artificial" groups. But then again, in the two such groups Freud does study in *Group Psychology*—the church and the army—"the individual's lack of freedom in a group" remains the principal phenomenon of group psychology.

Only one explanation, Freud hypothesizes, could account for this regressive, deindividuating potential in group life. Social rela-tions resemble nothing so much as they resemble relations of love. To these ties, Freud gives the name "the libidinal constitution of groups," which he explains as follows:

> love relationships (or, to use a more neutral expression, emotional ties) . . . constitute the essence of the group mind. . . . Our hy-pothesis finds support in the first instance from two passing thoughts. First, that a group is clearly held together by a power of some kind: and to what power could this feat be better ascribed than to Eros, which holds together everything in the world? Secondly, that if an individual gives up his distinctiveness in a group . . . , it gives one the impression that he does it because he feels the need of being in harmony with them rather than in opposition to them—so that perhaps after all he does it *"ihnen zu Liebe"* [for love of them].[23]

But the love relation is not *between* or *among* the members of the group. In Freud's problematic account, there is absent any direct relation among members at all. They seem strangers to one another, and what "unites" them is their focusing love and devotion on the same authority or leader and the real or imagined reciprocal receipt of love from that authority.

The existence of a leader as the focal point of love is a requirement of solidarity for any political group, claims Freud. Without it, common life suffers from the "psychological poverty" typical of the "present cultural state of America," where the

> bonds of a society are chiefly constituted by the identifications of its members with one another, while individuals of the leader type do not acquire the importance that should fall to them in the formation of a group.[24]

For a group to exist without a leader is apparently analogous to an individual without a superego: there is no synthesis or integrated "personality." No common life or shared sense of purpose emerges among the members of such a group. All that is accomplished is the "American" state of affairs: a group without a culture, without national identity, without a common character.[25]

Freud does not always insist that the ruler be a person or persons; the ruler can be an "idea or abstraction."[26] But it must be an abstraction the common man can envisage, identify with, feel emotional toward, and it must be an idea that can be shared widely across the population. For it is this sharing of the same love, this identification with the same leader or leading idea, that counteracts the centrifugal force of aggression and unites persons into a group.

But this process of erotic identification with the group, or state, should not be viewed as one between unchanged selves. At its best, the communal loyalty enters into and enriches the content of a person's moral voice, or superego. At its worst, the political identification simply overpowers and supplants the prior, individuating sense of conscience entirely. Group allegiances of the irrational, unreflective sort then emerge, as "*a number of individuals . . . put one and the same object in the place of their ego ideal. . . .*"[27]

Among persons for whom love of country has for all intents and purposes absorbed the potential opposition of individual conscience, Freud remarked that group life "appears to us as a revival of the primal horde."[28] And in terms that anticipate Arendt's critique of totalitarianism, *Group Psychology* describes the "group individual" left behind when erotic politics of the bad sort collapses

the space between persons we count upon in public, however much
we may strive to abolish it in private:

> [h]is liability to affect becomes extraordinarily intensified, while his in-
> tellectual ability is markedly reduced, both processes being evidently in
> the direction of an approximation to the other individuals in the
> group. . . .[29]

But to find that our personal identity is politically movable and
indeed comes to ''approximate'' the character of the community
in which we live is not necessarily to experience the kind of deindividuation Freud feared. Rousseau, for one, affirms the ethical
condition of a community wherein the common name of citizen
declares more about a person's identity than his given name. On
this view, the emergence of loyalties and convictions held in common with other persons is no surrender of an individuated moral
voice or will; instead it is a precondition of that will's taking on
general and ethical content beyond the parochialisms and pure
happenstance of self-interest. It is otherwise with the ''approxima-
tions'' of Freudian persons in groups because no community, no
common endeavor, no common name emerges among them at
all—only a parallel, mostly passive identification with an elevated
leader. Allegiance to an ethic so embodied in a source beyond our
influence is deindividuating because it replaces the particular will
of each, not with a more general will, but only with the equally
particular, surrogate will of the leader or leading class.

Freud's undressing of the state as a perverted ethical concept is
illuminating, but his overall vision of the grounds of political
solidarity seems indefensibly narrow, as is evident from his exclusive attention in *Group Psychology* to the church and the army
as examples of common life. Freud apparently felt no need to refer
to a wider spectrum of group types, because his argument comes
down to there being only one principle of authority for all human
associations, which is the father's authority and domination from
the primal horde on. We have by now so internalized love for that
kind of authority, from a long history of Oedipal guilt, that we
seek it out, we surrender to it, we fail in all attempts to rule as
brothers and equals.

Freud's argument takes its strength, as Marcuse put it, from the
way in which a concept such as the primal horde, however mythic,
gives economical expression to a long history of political authority
as domination. But Freud sometimes speaks as if groups without

leaders of the dominating sort are groups without solidity and authority at all—his disdain for "American ways" again. Against Freud, it is worth reiterating that political association at its best can know a form of authority and leadership beyond open or hidden domination of the one or few over the many. Aristotle's insistence on this particular point is enticing because of his agreement with Freud that prepolitical authority is always a matter of patriarchal domination. Families are monarchical in structure, not democratic, for Aristotle, and men are supposedly intended to rule women just as masters rule their slaves. The management of a household is always, therefore, exercise of authority over persons not one's equals, and hence an act of (benign) domination. But, notwithstanding his halting views on equality and family life, Aristotle recognized that life can be otherwise in the city; citizens can meet in public space as equals and form an association, a brother clan, on the basis of their perceived equality. Aristotle's own sense of who could count as equals in public remained sharply restrictive. But among the citizenry as he allowed it, politics spoke to the virtues of respect, admiration, and friendship among fellow countrymen. When such public emotions of solidarity are present, what Freud isolated in his account of Eros and the mechanics of group identification takes on a fundamentally different meaning. Aristotelian citizens come to form the "horizontal" identifications absent in Freud's hierarchical account of group psychology. *Qua* members, they experience themselves as sharing in a particular vision of the good life and associating in a common venture to preserve the city which secures that vision. Such a brotherhood can adopt a democratic, elegantly simple principle of authority relations—ruling and being ruled in turn. For when we perceive fellow citizens as implicated with us in a common vision and undertaking, then we can identify as like ourself whoever happens to be taking his term in office, just as we can all qualify to be that person in whom the rest of us see ourselves and our good. Solidarity, even the love (*philia*) of friendship is available through such horizontal ties, in place of the vertical tie Freud is in danger of making the sole source of political stability.

Even within Freud, the notion of erotic identification with authority is not exhausted by the description in *Group Psychology* of its hierarchical nature. As we shall see in later chapters, Freud counted on the erotic force of identification to do its work in therapy, to invest the analyst with his leadership role, to win over

Eros in service to cure. The potential for the patient's identification with the analyst to reenact the neurosis—"transference"—was worrisome to Freud, but at the same time he counted on his fellow analysts to stave off the invitation to become new father figures (or worse, sexual lovers). The authority of the analyst was instead to be an exercise in liberation of the patient from the dynamic which led to the transference and to new submissions to new father figures. But if such liberating authority and human association are available in therapy, they are in principle available in politics. Indeed, as was pointed out in the Introduction, there is a certain kind of human liberation that is simply unavailable outside of political community and attachment. The goods we seek or hold as private persons are there to know and hold in private, however much we may need to keep some sort of loose company with others to get them. But the common good is not something we can know apart from politics, apart from the deep loyalties that constitute a good in common. Not to turn from therapy to politics, therefore, is to remain a stranger to one's fellow citizens. It is to fail to understand that there are certain virtues of character the self cannot realize except through politics and allegiance to the common good.

The Aristotelian conception of political solidarity, friendship, and authority is not readily located in the modern nation-state. It is not only the sheer numbers involved that have destroyed the concept of the *polis* as an association in support of a common good. It is that liberal societies (at least) no longer believe in the notion of a *common* good at all. In the name of autonomy and pluralism, liberalism avows a thinner concept of community as a collection of individuals in pursuit of private goods and purposes, attracted together only through mutual need for protection and cooperation. In such a society, it is unlikely that the horizontal identifications and friendships sponsored by a *polis* can exist, and Freud's choice between the emptiness of "American" ties and the cohesion available through love as hypnotic surrender has its moment.

When Eros and politics go badly, in the frenzies of fatherlands and the perils of patriotism, they go badly in terms *Group Psychology* helps illumine. Eros is the gravest source of what has been called the "authoritarian personality." In such a character type, love of leader is so exalted as to obliterate an individual's superego entirely; national identifications of an irrational sort then sponsor a sense of belonging whose main characteristic is hatred of aliens, or outsiders. *Group Psychology* well analyzed this twisted political personality type before his coming to center stage. But Freud cannot adequately account for the fact that politics sometimes goes well, after all, and that when it does, Eros enriches rather than impoverishes personal character. It makes available to the self those civic virtues, such as solidarity, fellow-feeling and public mindedness, that are not present in a private life, no matter how liberated.

III

In one short paper written during the first World War and in a letter to Einstein in anticipation of the second, Freud set forth a series of musings about war and modern politics. In these essays Freud addresses two questions. The first concerns why war survives as a method of politics at all in so-called civilized nations. What appeal can it have for us? The second question is more historical and comparative: why is war not only alive and well, but, in Freud's view, getting worse all the time?

Freud's query as to "why war" is a limited one. He had no faith to lose in the rationality of the vast majority of persons and so takes no surprise from the attraction war holds for them, with its sanctioned overthrow of moral constraint and sudden allowance for instinctual, impulsive action. "When the community has no rebuke to make," Freud writes,

> there is an end of all suppression of the baser passions and men perpetrate deeds of cruelty, fraud, treachery and barbarity. . . .
> . . . .
> [I]ndividuals [will] permit themselves relief for a while from the heavy pressure of civilization . . . [will permit themselves] to grant a passing satisfaction to the instincts it holds in check.[30]

War, that is to say, is morally sanctioned instinctual liberation. It should surprise no one that if our morality is situated only in a faculty of conscience set *over* desire rather than *within* the kind of desires we have, then whenever conscience is clear about war, when Eros joins in by way of patriotism, there is available for "letting go" human instinctuality, raw, primal, unruly, cruel and sadistic. Throughout his war essays, Freud speaks about the "hypocrisy" war thus reveals about the civility of the ordinary citizen. But what he means by hypocrisy is the set of controls conscience represents:

> Anyone . . . compelled to act continually in the sense of precepts
> which are not the expression of instinctual inclinations, is living, psy-
> chologically speaking, beyond his means, and might objectively be
> designated a hypocrite . . . . It is undeniable that our [modern]
> civilization is extraordinarily favourable to the production of this form
> of hypocrisy. One might venture to say that it is based upon such
> hypocrisy and that it would have to submit to far-reaching modifica-
> tions if people were to undertake to live in accordance with the
> psychological truth. Thus there are very many more hypocrites then
> truly civilized persons . . . .[31]

But Freud thought this point about the mass appeal of war obvious on the one hand and misleading on the other. Mass psychology may support but rarely initiates war. At least as to 1914,
the question "why war" is properly put only to the statesmen who
made the decision, the leaders and authorities who played a
predominant role in releasing the conscience of the rest of us.
Here, Freud acknowledges that he had shared the general faith in
the enlightenment of the European intelligentsia:

> We had expected the great ruling powers among the white nations
> upon whom the leadership of the human species has fallen, who were
> known to have cultivated world-wide interests, to whose creative
> powers were due our technical advances . . . as well as the artistic and
> scientific acquisitions of the mind—peoples such as these we had ex-
> pected to succeed in discovering another way of settling misunder-
> standings and conflicts of interest.[32]

Freud was no pacifist and so presumably accepted that *some*
war decisions could be made by responsible statesmen, wholly
apart from any individual or collective urge to aggression. Indeed
Freud's own initial reaction to 1914 was, according to Jones, highly
partisan to Austria-Hungary.[33] But this reaction turned to disillu-
sion as the war dragged on, its purpose receded, and the carnage
mounted. Whatever the rationality of entrance into the war, its
subsequent course swept away all civilized constraints as even the
most cultured of statesmen "permit[ted] [themselves] every such
misdeed, every such act of violence as would disgrace the individual man."[34] Diplomacy degenerated from accepted and
perhaps necessary stratagems to a pure absence of ethical constraint
in the conduct of battle. The state "ignores the prerogatives of the
wounded and the medical service, the distinction between civil and
military sections of the population, . . . tramples in blind fury on
all that comes in its way . . . . "[35] The sad truth revealed in war-

time, then, according to Freud, is the more or less total hypocrisy of
the state itself as a sphere of moral progress. Like the primal father,
European leaders demand of the masses in peacetime restraints
they themselves have not fully internalized:

> the individual . . . has . . . a terrible opportunity to convince himself
> that . . . the state has forbidden to the individual the practice of
> wrong-doing, not because it desired to abolish it, but because it desires
> to monopolize it, like salt and tobacco. . . . [The state] absolves itself
> from the guarantees and contracts it had formed with other states, and
> makes unabashed confession of its rapacity and lust for power. . . . [36]

And every lust that the leadership frees itself to convert into a state
objective it calls upon the masses to "sanction in the name of
patriotism," knowing assuredly that there will always be political
appeal in a politics of war and the release from repression it offers.
Indeed the sorry dynamic between politics and war is how popular
war can be as a method of politics and hence how irresponsible
leaders can afford to be. Freud himself approached politics as a
sphere where leaders manipulate masses, but his analysis points
toward the reverse possibility as well: leadership penned in by, and
toadying to, a war hysteria not of its making. According to Jones,
Freud understood this hysteria of war all too well, experiencing
himself a kind of rejuvenation in 1914. Jones recounts that Freud
welcomed the hostilities "with useful enthusiasm, apparently a
reawakening of the military ardours of his boyhood." "All my
libido is given to Austro-Hungary," Freud declared. [37]

Freud's own attempt to explain the Great War's initial appeal
to himself is bizarre. What he insisted upon is that in an overly
repressive culture, war has the distinct advantage of restoring life
through death. Prior to the war, Freud had already echoed the
Nietzschean and Weberian criticism of modern life as impoverished, disenchanted, routinized. Not the least of the routiniza-
tions for Freud was the increasingly conventional and institutional
treatment of dying and death. It was as if, outside war, modern rational men and women no longer risked, wagered, or staked their
lives on any gamble. This

> has a powerful effect upon our lives. Life is impoverished, it loses in in-
> terest, when the highest stake in the game of living, life itself, [can] not
> be risked. It becomes as flat, as superficial, as one of those American
> flirtations in which it is from the first understood that nothing is to
> happen. . . . [38]

The appeal of war is to "sweep away this conventional treatment of death." Life during war regains its enchanted heroes, its opportunities for extraordinary behavior, for spontaneity, for pure release:

> People really are dying, and now not one by one, but many at a time, often ten thousand in a single day. . . . Life has, in truth, become interesting again; it has regained its full significance.[39]

There are not many passages in Freud where he sides so openly with the forces of instinctual liberation, and it is ironic to find such an endorsement in regard to war. But against the background of a culture that offered much repression and little gratification, ample security and little risk, Freud saw war's appeal, and in a manner of speaking, its ethical contribution, in the way it forced people once more to believe in death—and hence in living.

But if this is so, then war's psychological appeal cannot be understood narrowly in terms of an aggressive instinct. Freud's own remark regarding the giving of all his libido to Austria-Hungary points once more to the destructive, twisted potential of Eros as a political passion. Identifying patriotically with the leaders who sanctify war in the name of all that is good and true, citizens with no hatred of the enemy prepare to kill or be killed in the name of love of country.

Freud's second query about war concerns his sense that modern warfare is, if anything, more brutal in its conduct than wars fought in previous generations:

> Not only is it more . . . destructive than any war of other days, because of the enormously increased perfection of weapons . . . but it is at least as cruel, as embittered, as implacable as any that has preceded it. It sets at naught all those restrictions known as International Law, which in peace-time the states had bound themselves to observe. . . .[40]

In this passage, Freud is careful to distinguish between the technical advances that make war in 1914 more destructive than its predecessors and the psychological element of cruelty about it, in which it "at least" matches the bitterness and implacability of previous warfare. Freud's historical inquiries are directed to the latter, not the former, comparison: Granted that moderns still fight wars, why does the alleged progress in civilization not contribute to a moderation at least in the purposes and practices of battle? Why does the modern nation-state fight for "unconditional" surrender and "absolute" victory, whereas the Greek city-states, in Freud's understanding, limited the scope of their wars with one another by proclaiming that "no city of the league . . . be demolished, nor its olive-groves hewn down, nor its water cut off"?[41]

In answer to these questions, Freud offers his suspicion that the greater the instinctual repression society demands in peacetime, the more destructive the instinctual liberation achieved in war. Progress in civilization is therefore likely to be accompanied by progress in the horror of war. The frightening aspect of the Great War—what seemed new—was the vastness of the moral collapse it represented, the reckless abandon it now took to purge the civilized body of its overrepression. This was true, Freud lamented, from bottom to top of society, and no one, including himself, escaped some part in welcoming the purge in 1914.

In *Civilization and Its Discontents,* Freud compares the dangers of this situation with the "advantage which a comparatively small cultural group offers of allowing . . . [a] relatively harmless satisfaction of the inclination to aggression" against equally small neighbors.[42] The advantages were twofold. First, the smaller political units achieved a high degree of internal cohesion by redirecting hostile acts from citizen to foreigner. But they were also able to moderate their export of aggression through constant outlay in small feuds. Freud dubs this process the "narcissism of minor differences," and he refers to such examples as the Spanish and the Portuguese, the English and the Scotch. Each of these nations became a people partly by virtue of historical hostility to its neighbors. Freud also adds that the "Jew as stranger everywhere" has provided "most useful service" to this familiar fomenting of national identity through hostility to the intruder. Eros, here in the form of narcissistic identification with one's own tribe against the stranger, the foreigner, the alien, has thus long played its dark role in the history of politics and war. But this frequent expenditure of patriotic hostility against neighbor or stranger, while never pretty in previous generations, at least precluded the kind of mass build-up and sudden instinctual release that 1914 represents to Freud.

Having described the older, safety valve model of small and frequent feuding, Freud turns critically to the debased and destructive forms Eros takes when universalized, as when historically pressed into service to the ideal of the unity of Christiandom. The medieval efforts to unite as vast a unit as all of Christianity entailed an erotic identification so fierce within that unit as to breed extreme intolerance to those who dared remain outside the community of universal love. That is to say, the only form Eros could take in a community so large and artificial as universal Christianity was one whose major definition was by reference to the heretic.

Writing in 1930, Freud thought that modern warfare between large nation-states was destined to become more brutal in both the psychological and technical senses. The safety valve of small wars between small states seemed to be passing from the political scene: the sudden liberation from instinctual repression in one large world war was the horrible order of the day. And so long as Eros and politics mixed as badly as they had in the past, forging an artificial love within through hate without, war was likely to remain a prop of politics. In 1930 Freud speculated that this dynamic of aggression in service to national identity was likely to do its dirtiest work in two nations in particular:

> [T]he dream of a Germanic world-dominion called for anti-semitism as its complement; and it is intelligible that the attempt to establish a new, communist civilization in Russia should find its psychological support in the persecution of the bourgeois. One only wonders, with concern, what the Soviets will do after they have wiped out their bourgeois.[43]

Freud leaves these remarks and his theory of war psychology incomplete. But the implications of his views seem more ominous now than when written. For if nuclear technology means we must no longer have world war and if the political psychology of the nation-state still demands it, then we either have the world war we must not have or return to the more limited but frequent warfare Freud partly affirmed as basic to the older, more workable political order.

Chapter Five

Psychoanalysis and Religion

Freud's most insistent attempt to work out the cultural implications of psychoanalysis was in the area of religion. He devoted three book-length manuscripts to the origins and history of religion, including his first foray into the interpretation of culture (*Totem and Taboo*) and his last, posthumously published work (*Moses and Monotheism*). In between, Freud delivered his famous broadside at the truth of religion (*The Future of an Illusion*) and returned to the worrisome question of man's religiosity at the start of *Civilization and Its Discontents*.

Why religion, again and again? For Freud, religion represented the central elaboration of public meaning for the human species to date, and yet the epitome of untruth as revealed by the advent of psychoanalysis. Freud's tone, cool and impartial elsewhere, is fiery, even combative on the coming clash between science and religion and on the inevitable triumph psychoanalysis makes possible over the "neurotic" or "infantile" phase of civilization. This triumph will be psychoanalysis' greatest cultural achievement; it will accomplish science's "appointed task" of reconciling man to civilization, but it will also unleash new dangers of nihilism. For if the existence of God is the "sole reason" that keeps persons from murdering their neighbors, then his death will surely provoke an un-bounded reign of terror. And if hitherto it has taken a God to make nature meaningful, then when the world is disenchanted of belief, the question of whether science in place of religion can make life intelligible will come to the fore.

Freud typically scoffed at "the idea of life having a purpose. ..." "Nobody," he taunted, "talks about the purpose of the life of animals," and the presumption that humans are uniquely cre-ated with some *telos,* or goal, in mind, "stands and falls with the religious system."[1] In humbling man's presumptive uniqueness, Freud saw himself as following in the footsteps of Copernicus and Darwin—psychoanalysis as the "third" great "blow" to "the self-love of humanity."[2] The Copernican revolution dismantled the "cosmological illusion" by which man "naively" placed himself at the center of creation; Darwinism put an end to man's arrogant claim to a "divine descent" and reinstituted the "bond of com-munity between [man] and the animal kingdom." And psycho-analysis inflicted the "most wounding" blow of all—the news that "the ego is not master in its own house."[3] The prior two revolu-tions had already made it difficult for persons to understand them-selves according to the testament of Genesis. But it was psycho-analysis alone which recovered the hidden unconscious origins of religion itself and, in so doing, concluded the battle against cul-ture's most powerful fiction.

I

Freud himself understood there was an important duality in his ap-proach to the psychology of religion. He is best known, through the title of *The Future of an Illusion,* for debunking religion as springing purely from the individual's infantile motives for wish-ing God the Benevolent Father into existence. This is an important aspect of Freud's case against religion, but he combined it, espe-cially in *Moses and Monotheism,* with a historical argument fore-shadowed by his earlier inquiries into totemism. On this argu-ment, religion is an illusion which is at the same time an act of historical recollection, a way of recalling deeply buried truths about the fearful, criminal origins of civilization. And when this latent historical content of religion is recomprehended, then its full Oedipal structure is also revealed in the two faces God wears—benevolence and vengeance.

In *The Future of an Illusion,* Freud develops the nonhistorical side of his argument against religious fiction as follows:

God is our own creation, an illusion we believe in precisely because it illustrates the world according to our infantile liking. Religion is the adult's last and lasting attempt at flight from nasty reality back into infantile fantasy, at conjuring up a world of make-believe we have no right to believe in but want to believe in very badly. God, heaven, life after death—these are psychological creations whose existence can be understood only in terms of the motives we have for inventing them. The very power of faith to ignore reason (*Credo quia absurdum*) indicates we are dealing with a set of ideas humanity must have the deepest of motives for believing. But, as is typical of Freud, these deep motives are rooted in material, not spiritual, puzzlement and perplexity. As I have pointed out previously and need only summarize here, early childhood is mired in the anxiety implicit in being dependent on the help of others to satisfy basic needs. Within the family, the child learns that instinctual satisfaction depends on parental mediation. The parents, and especially the perceived stronger father, are figures of protection to be relied on. The father is the hero combatant of the child's fears. And the infant's fearsome helplessness lasts long enough for a dependent mentality to take hold: the expectancy that parental care will reappear to conquer fear whenever fear appears.

This desire to be fathered proves difficult to give up. To face the world on one's own; to admit to the impersonality and hostility of natural forces; to reconcile oneself to a world under no one's loving control—for all these admissions the sheltered child is ill prepared. Far easier, in later life and new situations of fear and perplexity, to respond according to the infantile prototype—to personalize nature into a world of father deities:

> When the growing individual finds that he is destined to remain a child for ever, that he can never do without protection against strange superior powers, he lends those powers the features belonging to the figure of his father; he creates for himself the gods whom he dreads, whom he seeks to propitiate, and whom he nevertheless entrusts with his own protection. Thus his longing for a father is a motive identical with his need for protection against the consequences of his human weakness. The defence against childish helplessness is what lends its characteristic features to the adult's reaction to the helplessness which *he* has to acknowledge—a reaction which is precisely the formation of religion.[4]

In the personification of nature, wishing plays the largest part; we make nature over into what we would like it to be, into what it seemed to the child's eye. The origin of God, like the origin of our dreams, is in wish fulfillment; in fact, one might say God is a dream answering to humanity's "oldest, strongest and most urgent wishes. . . ."[5]

Freud's account of the psychological motives for religious belief has been criticized for slipping back into the "unsociological" Enlightenment view of religion as wholly irrational, an isolable error without functional relation to any part of the social world. But, despite the title of his most famous book on the subject, Freud knew religion is, or at least was, a functional illusion. He recognized, though he stood against, the use of religion to sanctify obedience to social authority. And he was interested, from early in his career until his last written work, in the latent, or historical, content of religion. "God," Freud wrote, "must be recognized as a memory—a distorted one, it is true, but nevertheless a memory." But, like a neurotic symptom, God cannot withstand conscious knowledge of his origins. To know the psychology of religion is to know why it is false.

On the subject of religion's historical origin, Freud adopted from Darwin and from anthropologists of his time the description of rudimentary human groups—"hordes"—organized around worship of a sacred animal, or "totem." The horde expressed its unity in terms of the common descent of clan members from the totem animal, whose slaughter was ordinarily prohibited on pain of death. Nevertheless, once a year worship of the totem would be temporarily suspended in favor of its ritual slaughter and ingestion.

The horde's sense of common descent was accompanied by the first appearance of the incest taboo in history, all members refraining from sexual relations with one another.[6] No one can overlook, Freud writes, that these two prohibitions—neither to kill the totem nor to have sexual relations with a woman of the same totem— "coincide in their content with the two crimes of Oedipus . . . , as well as with the two primal wishes of children, the insufficient repression or the re-awakening of which forms the nucleus of perhaps every psychoneurosis."[7] This first worship of a "sacred" creature must be understood as a collective symptom, a screen expressing in disguised form the repressed memory of the murder and overthrow of the father by the brothers of the horde ("primal crime"). The purpose of the symptom is to allay, by disguising, the sense of guilt caused by that memory. In totemic thought, the clan absolves its guilt for the original father murder by exalting the substitute animal into a god and prohibiting any repetition of its murder. (Freud's analysis of dreams and neurosis had long since revealed to him the use of animals by the unconscious to symbolize the father.) Simultaneously, the totemic law of exogamy punishes the sexual motive behind the father murder.

Alongside his account of the early religion of totemism, Freud late in life added an account of the Oedipal grounding of monotheism among the Jews. Monotheism represents a quantum leap over totemism in the social history of guilt—and in the progress of both culture and neurosis. Nowhere does Freud write more sympathetically about religion than when dealing with the achievements monotheism made possible among the Jews. But nowhere does he make clearer the intimacy of those achievements with neurosis.

Monotheism is the highest form the religion of the father can assume. The animal gods have become humanized, the competing forces ousted, and God the Father stands alone, omnipotent and omniscient, the Almighty Being. With monotheism, it would seem that the repressed memory of the primal father has returned to a remarkable degree and wears its most transparent disguise. Only "thus was it that the supremacy of the father of the primal horde was re-established and that the emotions relating to him could be repeated."[8]

What happened among the Jews to make them the first full bearers of humanity's repressed father complex? What happened, says Freud in his largest tribute to the historical force of a single individual, was Moses. In Freud's interpretation, Moses was a lieutenant of the Pharoah Ikhanaton, whose attempt to impose a monotheistic religion on the Egyptians themselves proved abortive; after Ikhanaton's overthrow and death, Moses carried on the experiment among the formerly enslaved Jews, escaping into exile with them when a new dynasty turned hostile to his and Ikhanaton's ideas.

For a time, Moses' campaign proved successful—until the more primitive Jews rose up against his enlightened despotism and murdered him. Freud takes the biblical story of Moses' not being allowed by God into the promised land as a vague indication of the more earthly punishment Moses suffered. After their rebellion, the Jews lapsed from monotheism for a time, adopting the worship of the local deities of the Sinai peninsula—in particular the Midianite god Jahve.

But over a generation or more—perhaps the forty years in the wilderness—the Mosaic ideals returned to convert Jahve into the one and only God. And the Jews have remained with the Mosaic God ever since, a record of religious survival unparalleled in the West.

The peculiar fate of the Jews, then, the fate that determined them as history's first monotheists, was the repetition of the primal crime in regard to Moses. The killing of the founder made their Oedipal guilt twice born, and decreed that the repressed phylogenetic memory of father murder should haunt them most closely:

> It would be worth while to understand how it was that the monotheist idea made such a deep impression precisely on the Jewish people and that they were able to maintain it so tenaciously. It is possible, I think, to find an answer. Fate had brought the great deed and misdeed of primaeval days, the killing of the father, closer to the Jewish people by causing them to repeat it on the person of Moses, an outstanding father-figure. It was a case of "acting out" instead of remembering, as happens so often with neurotics during the work of analysis.[9]

Jewish monotheism, then, symbolically represents the return of the repressed in collective life; and the repressed returns just as it does in neurosis. After a period of forgetfulness—Freud calls it a latency period—the memory of Moses (and through him of the primal crime) brushes consciousness, only to be repressed again via the suitable disguises provided by monotheistic culture.

For the Jews, monotheism was a mixed blessing. On the one hand, their "progress in spirituality" was nonpareil for the times. The prohibition of idolatry, for example, helped to subordinate sense perception to abstract ideas as they built their culture on the unpictured concept of God. This enforced a stunning intellectual advancement on Jewish culture:

> The new realm of intellectuality was opened up, in which ideas, memories and inferences became decisive in contrast to the lower psychical activity which had direct perceptions by the sense-organs as its content. This was unquestionably one of the most important stages on the path to hominization.[10]

But Freud's affirmation of the progressive role of religion is halting, qualified always by his insistence that the history of monotheism is also the history of neurosis. For monotheism was a stinging and symptomatic expression among the Jews of guilty conscience: since they had sinned against their God, their religion could be only a perpetual piece of atonement—an atonement which could never placate the sense of guilt because the source of the guilt remained unacknowledged. This religion of permanent expiation the Prophets especially were to enforce upon the people, driving the Jews toward what Freud calls insatiable "transports of moral asceticism" and "ethical heights" of instinctual renunciation unknown in antiquity. The exhortations of the Prophets "possess the characteristic—uncompleted and incapable of completion—of obsessional neurotic reaction-formations."[11]

The obsessive character of religion, Freud notes, "is in the nature of an axiom." From the time he first studied totemism,

> I have never doubted that religious phenomena are only to be understood on the pattern of the individual neurotic symptoms familiar to us —as the return of long since forgotten, important events in the primaeval history of the human family—and that they have to thank precisely this origin for their compulsive character and that, accordingly, they are effective on human beings by force of the historical truth of their content.[12]

The obsessive nature of religion is crucial to Freud's point of view, for this is where the power of religion lies. Suppose one were to consider religion merely a "tradition" passed on from generation to generation by oral or written communication. Such a tradition "would be listened to, judged, and perhaps dismissed, like any other piece of information from outside; it would never attain the privilege of being liberated from the constraint of logical thought."[13] Communication from the outside simply cannot account for either the continuity of religious culture or the remarkable hold that concepts beyond empirical experience have had on the human mind.

Religion, like any deeply seated part of culture, must be passed on internally; the concept of God must be an external manifestation, a symptom of an unconscious memory obsessively plaguing human beings. There must be some experience whose memory God obliquely expresses. That experience is the primal crime, the murder of the father. This memory "must have undergone the fate of being repressed, the condition of lingering in the unconscious, before it is able to display such powerful effects on its return, to bring the masses under its spell. . . ."[14] Religion accomplishes on a wider social scale what obsessive neurosis does for individuals: it uses illusion and fantasies to mask the threatened return of the repressed.

In Freud's treatment, Christianity forms a validating sequel to his interpretation of monotheism and the social origins of guilt. In a most intriguing way, Christian doctrine comes close to healing our obsession, replacing guilt with salvation precisely because it implicitly acknowledges—and absolves us from—the original source of human remorse. Christ the Son delivers man from his sins by laying down his life in expiation. What, then, must the original sin have been that demanded the son's life in return, if not the murder of the father?

> Paul, a Roman Jew from Tarsus, seized upon this sense of guilt and traced it back correctly to its original source. He called this the "original sin"; it was a crime against God and could only be atoned for by death. With the original sin death came into the world. In fact this crime deserving death had been the murder of the primal father who was later deified. But the murder was not remembered: instead of it there was a phantasy of its atonement, and for that reason this phantasy could be hailed as a message of redemption (*evangelium*). A son of God had allowed himself to be killed without guilt and had thus taken on himself the guilt of all men. It had to be a son, since it had been the murder of a father.[15]

The ambivalence of the father complex, however, permeates Christian doctrine also. Meant to propitiate the murdered father, the murdered son nevertheless dethrones the father once again and creates a new religion in his own image.

In what sense do actual historical events lie behind the origins of religion and the rise of monotheism? I have argued previously that the dubious empirical status of the phylogenetic hypothesis is wrapped up with Freud's attempt to account for the universality of infantile Oedipal experiences by postulating actual Oedipal crimes in the primal horde, memory of which is somehow inherited by children. Doubt about such a hypothesis rested both on the impossibility of explaining how memory of actual events could be inherited and also on the absence of independent evidence for the occurrence of the alleged primal crime.

In *Totem and Taboo,* Freud seems to recognize these difficulties. He comes down only tentatively on the side of the primal crime as a historical event, "without laying claim to any finality of judgment. . . ."[16] An alternative account is equally plausible. The mere hostile *impulse* against the father, the mere existence of a wishful *fantasy* of killing and devouring him, "would have been enough to produce the moral reaction that created totemism and taboo." [17]

Freud's writings on religion and history here reach a moment in 1912 parallel to what he had experienced at the turn of the century with his analysis of hysterics. Although he first regarded his patients' tales of childhood seduction or abuse as literal recollections, Freud finally came to believe he was dealing with unconscious wishes creating fantasies with all the force of reality to the patient. After this moment, psychoanalysis as theory as well as therapy centered on an "explanation of the stability, efficacity and relatively coherent nature of the subject's phantasy life." [18]

Freud's final response to whether he is dealing with fact or fantasy on the historical level is revealing and in accord with the argument put forward earlier against Freud's reliance on mythological prehistory. "[T]he distinction, which may seem fundamental to other people, does not in our judgment affect the heart of the matter." [19] In the beginning could be either the deed or the dream. If the brothers actually killed their father repeatedly in history, that, coupled with their ambivalence about such acts, would serve to explain the remorse that drove them toward the prohibitions of totemism. On the other hand, if our primitive ancestors, like today's children, only fancied the Oedipal crimes, those fantasies would still have been historically real and powerful; they would still have served to conjure up guilt and the Oedipal contents of religion. To call something a fantasy in psychoanalysis is not at all to dismiss it as unreal, a mistake, a powerless illusion.

II

Religion, for Freud, always remained the clearest example of culture's own illness, an accepted way of being moral and social which psychoanalysis nevertheless finds objectionable. Religion qualifies as the deepest social obstacle to human liberation. Just as an individual hides from reality inside his neurotic symptoms, so a whole people hides through its rituals, personifications, and anthropomorphisms. The collective repression of the Oedipal complex is no better than its individual repression. Both lead to a guilty refusal to acknowledge, let alone transform, the aggressive and sexual attractions of humanity. Religious pacification of guilt is an endless, obsessive repetition of the infantile attitude toward the father.

And yet one positive aspect of a communal neurosis is that it saves individuals the trouble of manufacturing their own personal sickness. Religion can, and once did, stave off guilt as well as foment it. Religion can save as well as condemn. This dual nature of religion's relation to guilt can be seen in the split which opened between the theory and practice of Calvinism, as outlined by Max Weber in his classic *The Protestant Ethic and the Spirit of Capitalism.* As a doctrine, Calvin's notion of predestination could succeed only in aggravating man's anxiety on the question of salvation. What after all could represent more of a return of guilt in history than the notion of the inscrutable, unreachable God who wills our fate freely without regard to our actions? In parish practice, however, Calvinism came to offer more certain knowledge of one's salvation from sin—through the "election" signified by the ascetic but energetic pursuit of one's worldly tasks. To be a Calvinist in practice was to be a member of a group who reinforced each other's sense of mutual salvation. Calvinism may have created anxious minds, but anxious minds also adopted Calvinism to salve their own anxiety.

But in his own age and among his patients, Freud thought that religious illusion was no longer even a saving lie. Religious culture in a scientific age had little imperative value, provided none of the old psychological reassurances. To the contrary: Freud saw nothing as more responsible for aggravating his patients' private neuroses than the dogmas of the priests. Religion had now gone over entirely to the side of guilt, demanding instinctual renunciation while providing no compensatory feeling of grace. Freud's patients lived in the worst of all possible religious worlds, a hypocritical one where churches extracted guilt without belief, obedience but not faith. And the force of religion sans faith is the force of repression outright.

There was no question in Freud's mind that humanity's long experiment with religion was ending and was ending in failure. This prolonged infantile answer to the nature of the universe, this mass delusion, this "neurotic phase" of civilization, had been dealt a fatal blow by empirical science and by psychoanalysis itself. Phrases which make the project of human liberation depend on the abolition of religion abound in Freud. Religion and its techniques are "neurotic relics," "an historical residue."[20] A "turning-away from religion is bound to occur with the fatal inevitability of a process of growth. . . . ''[21] Its "infantilism is destined to be surmounted.''[22]

What makes religion the "infantile phase" of culture is its refusal to accept nature as a realm of law and necessity, its escape instead into the omnipotence of a God. Freud's irreverent sense of freedom leads him to replace God the Almighty with another god, known by its ancient name:

> Our God [Logos] will fulfill whichever . . . wishes nature outside us allows, but he will do it very gradually, only in the unforeseeable future, and for a new generation of men. He promises no compensation for us, who suffer grievously from life.[23]

Logos and *Ananke* (necessity): these become the only guardians of nature Freud himself would allow. Resignation to natural law replaces the consolation of faith as psychoanalysis replaces religion. Here, Freud takes as his model the great Leonardo da Vinci. Leonardo the master painter and scientist was also a spiritual man in the sense that he expressed awe at the wonder of creation. But his appeal to Freud lies in his refusal to explore this awe through a personal relation with God. "The reflections in which he has recorded the deep wisdom of his last years of life breathe the resignation of the human being who subjects himself to . . . the laws of nature, and who expects no alleviation from the goodness or grace of God.''[24]

For Freud, nothing essential attaches culture to conventional religion any longer; we have nothing to lose but our illusions. Those Cassandras who counsel caution, who tell us only religion keeps the masses in line, who predict the end of culture with the end of religion, have it backward. With the alleged truth out about God, Freud sees civilization running a greater risk if it maintains the present attitude toward religion than if it gives it up altogether.[25] The "great mass of the uneducated and oppressed," Freud writes, already "have every reason for being enemies of civilization.''[26] When they hear of God's death,

> [i]s there not a danger here that the hostility of these masses to civilization will throw itself against the weak spot that they have found in their task-mistress? If the sole reason why you must not kill your neighbour is because God has forbidden it and will severely punish you for it in this or the next life—then, when you learn that there is no God and that you need not fear His punishment, you will certainly kill your

neighbour without hesitation, and you can only be prevented from doing so by mundane force. Thus either these dangerous masses must be
held down most severely and kept most carefully away from any chance
of intellectual awakening, or else the relationship between civilization
and religion must undergo a fundamental revision.[27]

The "fundamental revision" for which Freud speaks is the passage
of humanity from religious morality to rational ethics. All those instinctual renunciations that religion has traditionally enforced—
we must publish the reasons for them or let them perish:

> [W]e may now argue that the time has probably come, as it does in an
> analytic treatment, for replacing the effects of repression by the results
> of the rational operation of the intellect. We may foresee, but hardly
> regret, that such a process of remoulding will not stop at renouncing
> the solemn transfiguration of cultural precepts, but that a general revi-
> sion of them will result in many of them being done away with. In this
> way our appointed task of reconciling men to civilization will to a great
> extent be achieved.[28]

How, then, are we to bring about, on a large scale, a morality of
reason rather than repression? This is the great task psychoanalysis
can yet set itself. But before following Freud in his attempt to
outline how the "rational operation of intellect" would work, we
must note Freud's questionable assumption that religion and rationality are mutually exclusive categories.

Consider, by way of analogy, Freud's discussion of the psychology of love. Like the devout meeting God, lovers meet in a thicket
of Oedipal motives. At times, Freud wields the category of motives
to make love sound hopelessly pathological or "duplicitous," in
Rieff's term—as when Freud writes that we are condemned to love
only those who resemble ourselves or our mothers or fathers.

Suppose a person were to ask Freud, "What will happen to my
love of my spouse if you convince me my motives for seeking out
this relationship are deviously Oedipal?" Freud could not answer
for certain. It might be that a lover could not embrace his or her
former feelings once the motive for loving had become clarified.
But it is also possible and even likely that the person's motives do
not exhaust the love, that grounds of love exist capable of surviving
conscious and rational reflection on how the love began. If this
were not conceded by Freud, then he would have no psychology,
only a psychopathology of love.

Freud's conclusions ought to be similar in regard to religion
and its relation to human freedom. One form of religion—the

neurotic form—cannot withstand psychoanalysis, any more than could the deathly form of conscience Freud traced out in individuals. Once revealed, the Oedipal obsession with God the Father becomes unstable, and the believer finds his faith, to this extent, groundless. In debunking these motives for religion, Freud thus classically aids our search for freedom as independence, for autonomous action and a break with the "authority of the past."

But all this does not mean there could not remain grounds for continued belief in religion even after our motives for belief became transparent. There could be, this is to assert, a form of religious commitment whose basis we could consciously affirm. Freud typically does not allow for this. He writes as if rationality demands a strict choice between itself and any form of religious attachment.

At the beginning of *Civilization and Its Discontents*, Freud takes up this question of rationally reconstructed religion. The subject matter of *The Future of an Illusion*, he acknowledges, was limited to

> what the common man understands by his religion— . . . the system of doctrines and promises which on the one hand explains to him the riddles of this world with enviable completeness, and, on the other, assures him that a careful Providence will watch over his life and will compensate him in a future existence for any frustrations he suffers here.[29]

Philosophers and large numbers of others sense that *such* a religion is untenable but "nevertheless try to defend it piece by piece in a series of pitiful rearguard actions." They "think they can rescue the God of religion by replacing him with an impersonal, shadowy and abstract principle. . . ." But

> [t]he common man cannot imagine . . . Providence otherwise than in the figure of an enormously exalted father. Only such a being can understand the needs of the children of men and be softened by their prayers and placated by the signs of their remorse. The whole thing is so patently infantile, so foreign to reality, that to anyone with a friendly attitude to humanity it is painful to think that the great majority of mortals will never be able to rise above this view of life.[30]

Thus Freud shunts aside the question of rational commitment to religion as simply not relevant to what gives religion its mass appeal. At the same time, in *Civilization and Its Discontents*, Freud returns to the question of whether he has gotten the origins of this mass appeal right in his prior works. He recounts the response of a

friend to whom he had sent a copy of *The Future of an Illusion*.
While "entirely agree[ing] with my judgment upon religion,"
Freud writes,

> he was sorry I had not properly appreciated the true source of religious
> sentiments. This . . . consists in a peculiar feeling, which he himself is
> never without, which he finds confirmed by many others, and which he
> may suppose is present in millions of people. It is a feeling which he
> would like to call a sensation of "eternity," a feeling as of something
> limitless, unbounded—as it were, "oceanic." This feeling, he adds, is
> a purely subjective fact, not an article of faith; it brings with it no
> assurance of personal immortality, but it is the source of the religious
> energy which is seized upon by the various Churches and religious sys-
> tems. . . . One may, he thinks, rightly call oneself religious on the
> ground of this oceanic feeling alone, even if one rejects every belief and
> every illusion.[31]

Freud begins his public response to this friendly criticism cau-
tiously. He "cannot discover this 'oceanic' feeling" in himself,
and it "is not easy to deal scientifically with feelings." But "this
gives me no right to deny that [this feeling] does in fact occur in
other people." What, then, does the feeling referred to consist in?

> If I have understood my friend rightly, he means . . . a feeling of an in-
> dissoluble bond, of being one with the external world as a whole. . . .
> [He means] an intimation of [one's] connection with the world . . .
> through an immediate feeling. . . .[32]

But even granted the reality of such oceanic sensation, the notion
that it is primary and irreducible ("immediate") is an interpretation psychoanalysis disputes and dares to challenge with its prefer-
ence for genetic explanations. In religion, just as in love, oceanic
feelings of the above sort are traceable back to an early stage of
"ego-feeling" that must have accompanied the infant's as yet
blurry sense of its distinction from the external world. And if

> we may assume that there are many people in whose mental life this
> primary ego-feeling has persisted to a greater or less degree, it would
> exist in them side by side with the narrower and more sharply demar-
> cated ego-feeling of maturity, like a kind of counterpart to it. In that
> case, the ideational contents appropriate to it would be precisely those
> of limitlessness and of a bond with the universe—the same ideas with
> which my friend elucidated the "oceanic" feeling.[33]

So explained as but an infantile relic irretrievable within the
bounds set by the reality principle, the use of oceanic feelings to

console man with the conventionally religious notion of eternity once again stands exposed, as Freud's friend had already acknowledged. However, Freud was not content to leave his response to his friend at this. For the notion that religious need is at bottom a need to retrieve a state of intimate attachment with others carries with it a hidden affirmation of religion, stripped of its illusions and mythic elaborations. Thus Freud characteristically disputes the claim of oceanic feelings to be the source of religiosity; "the part played by the oceanic feeling . . . is ousted from a place in the foreground" by the even stronger need which Freud had isolated in *The Future of an Illusion* and which he now reiterates to his friend:

> [A] feeling can only be a source of energy if it is itself the expression of a strong need. The derivation of religious needs from the infant's helplessness and the longing for the father aroused by it seems to me incontrovertible, especially since the feeling is not simply prolonged from childhood days, but is permanently sustained by fear of the superior power of Fate. I cannot think of any need in childhood as strong as the need for a father's protection. . . . Thus . . . [t]he origin of the religious attitude can be traced back in clear outlines as far as the feeling of infantile helplessness. . . . There may be something further behind that, but for the present it is wrapped in obscurity.[34]

Comprehended as parasitic on the theme of infantile helplessness, religion lacks its affirmative moment; it stands revealed in Freud's mind as pejoratively perpetuated infantilism.

In and of itself, Freud's rejection of religion might not be of much import in our modern scientific age. What is of more concern is the ideal of human liberation behind the rejection. Freud stands in danger of reducing all our moral and political beliefs, all our allegiances and felt belongings, to the infantile-obsessive sort. Whether in his psychology of love or politics or religion, we have seen Freud always at least partly sour about the need for consolation or "oceanic feeling." Psychoanalysis enters upon the scene in the name of resignation to a reality that offers no final deliverance from our sufferings.

But as is typical in Freud, an affirmative teaching breaks through his own resigned pessimism. In the same year as *Civilization and Its Discontents'* publication, *Totem and Taboo* received its first Hebrew translation. Freud added a surprising and moving preface to this edition, which begins as follows:

> No reader [of the Hebrew version of] this book will find it easy to put himself in the emotional position of an author who is ignorant of the

language of holy writ, who is completely estranged from the religion of his fathers—as well as from every other religion—and who cannot take a share in nationalist ideals, but who has yet never repudiated his people, who feels that he is in his essential nature a Jew and who has no desire to alter that nature. If the question were put to him: "Since you have abandoned all these common characteristics of your countrymen, what is there left to you that is Jewish?" he would reply: "A very great deal, and probably its very essence."[35]

This passage makes clear that Freud's attitude toward the survival of his own religious identity after God's death is more complex than his theory allowed. About himself, Freud understood that his complete estrangement from "the religion of his fathers" did not likewise estrange him from the religious loyalties and identifications that had long since become implicated in his own identity. Even as atheist and nonnationalist, Freud affirmed the virtue of his earthly, political bond to his "people," his "countrymen." The very "essence" of Judaism as a common identity survived God, and Freud had no desire to "repudiate" but on the contrary affirmed the "common characteristics" among Jews he could not abandon without at the same time abandoning deep parts of himself.

For Freud to recognize autobiographically that religious conviction and communal loyalty play a positive role in giving content and depth to a human character is for him to draw back from his usual tone of mistrust about communal feelings, whether of the religious or political variety. As on all questions of "psychosynthesis," Freud thus finally gives no determinate answer on the earthly future of religion. The "religion of the fathers," the religion of mass appeal: these forms Freud thought he had analyzed in a way that rendered them bankrupt. But he leaves open the possibility that others will follow his own example in discovering a rational allegiance to their defining religious tradition, even after being psychoanalytically dispossessed of their infantile forms of faith.

Chapter Six

Sublimation: A Way Out?

With the boldest of claims Freud introduces sublimation in his 1914 *Papers on Metapsychology* as an alternative ethic to religion and repression: "sublimation is a way out, a way by which [the claims of the ego] can be met *without* involving repression."[1] After such an opening statement, it is surprising that there follows no sustained Freudian commentary on sublimation. As Ricoeur puts it, "in Freud's written work the notion of sublimation is both fundamental and episodic."[2] In their recent reexamination of Freud's metapsychology, Yankelovich and Barrett reach a similar conclusion: "psychoanalysts have always had trouble with sublimation. . . . It flickers waywardly in and out of Freud's writings. . . ."[3]

What we do find in Freud is an expression of the compensatory, or "economical," difference between repression and sublimation.[4] Repression is an uneconomical form of ego defense in that it imprisons the instinctual demand in the unconscious, fixing it at its primal level and providing no outlet for the instinctual energy it represents. The repressed demand then "ramifies like a fungus," taking on an "extraordinary and dangerous strength" due to the lack of energy expenditure. It exerts a "continuous straining in the direction of consciousness." The result is that repression must increase its countervailing pressure, thereby placing a constant drain on the mind's resources. Neurotic symptoms stem from this conflict, providing a disguise through which the energy attached to the repressed demand can be discharged without acknowledging the *meaning* of the demand. "A symptom is a sign of, and a substitute for, an instinctual satisfaction . . . ; it is a consequence of the process of repression."[5]

Freud can therefore conclude that "economically, [repression's] abrogation denotes a saving."[6] Its replacement by the nonrepressive defense known as sublimation would allow for the redirected investment of libido in social tasks rather than its mere damming up and occasional outlet in unproductive symptoms.

I

In Freud's first published use of the term "sublimation," in *Three Essays on the Theory of Sexuality* (1905), the economic aspect is at the fore, part and parcel of a genetic explanation of cultural activity as derivative from primal instinctual demands. Sublimation is defined in 1905 as the diversion or deflection of energy from sexual use to other ends.[7] In particular the displacement is of the pregenital components of infantile sexuality. Given that we must, as a species, continue to expend sexual energy in reproduction, it is the pregenital components that provide a free-floating pool of energy available for redirection and sublimation. If this can be done, "a not inconsiderable increase in psychical efficiency results. . . ."[8] And "[h]istorians of civilization appear to be at one in assuming that powerful components are acquired for every kind of cultural achievement by this diversion of sexual instinctual forces from sexual aims. . . ."[9]

But understood only as a socially functional way of expending instinctual energy sublimation is a highly unsatisfying aspect of Freud's theory. In the first place, Freud has hardly yet explained what distinguishes the instinctual diversions of sublimation from those of repression. Each alike depends on *desexualizing* the aim and object of libido and contenting human beings with so-called secondary activity, or "substitute gratifications." As Yankelovich and Barrett conclude, sublimation is "never quite separated from the repression or suppression of instinctual[ity]. . . . "[10] That is to say, sublimation is as repressive of instinctuality (in the common meaning of "repressive") as is repression (considered as a special process of defense). This underlying resemblance in the two processes of desexualization is one reason why Freud's attitude toward sublimation is ambiguous, why he is never far from treating cultural formation as analogous to symptom formation in a neurosis:

> If the development of civilization has such a far reaching similarity to the development of the individual and if it employs the same methods, may we not be justified in reaching the diagnosis that, under the influence of cultural urges, some civilizations, or some epochs of civilization—possibly the whole of mankind—have become neurotic?[11]

Moreover, the compensatory libidinal economics suggested by sublimation leads to a mountainous problem in psychoanalytic theory upon introduction of the death instinct. In the key *Papers on Metapsychology,* Freud had connected his early remarks on sublimation with his new research into narcissism—specifically the way in which the ego can lay hold of libido directed toward objects and redirect it internally as "narcissistic libido." Such transformation

> obviously implies an abandonment of sexual aims, a desexualization—a kind of sublimation, therefore. Indeed, the question arises, and deserves careful consideration, whether this is not the universal road to sublimation, whether all sublimation does not take place through the mediation of the ego, which begins by changing sexual object-libido into narcissistic libido and then, perhaps, goes on to give it another aim.[12]

In other words, the ability to sublimate is now seen as depending on the prior creation of a "displaceable and neutral energy"—"the narcissistic store of libido, that is desexualized Eros"—to which the ego can then assign social aims. But if culture taps into and makes use of human instinctual energy only by first desexualizing it, then culture has the ironic result of unbalancing the instinctual economy of human beings in favor of aggression. Freud attends to this implication in *The Ego and The Id:*

> By thus getting hold of the libido from the object-cathexes, setting itself up as sole love-object, and desexualizing or sublimating the libido of the id, the ego is working in opposition to the purposes of Eros and placing itself at the service of the opposing instinctual impulses.
>
> . . . .
>
> After sublimation the erotic component no longer has the power to bind the whole of the destructiveness that was combined with it, and

this is released in the form of an inclination to aggression and destruction.[13]

On the level of instinctual economics, therefore, sublimation is
hardly a "way out." Sharing responsibility with repression for the
desexualization of human interests, sublimation must also share
responsibility for the fact that the triumph of Eros over aggression
in our cultural lives is by no means assured. Unless there is some
other way to enliven Eros, desexualization is always a threat to its
balance of power over the death instinct.

These difficulties with sublimation have led many of Freud's
followers to dispense with the concept altogether, thereby returning cultural activity to its autonomous, heavenly location. A recent
example of this approach is the conclusion of Yankelovich and Barrett: "It would, perhaps, be better to put more emphasis on the
new [mental] structure itself—its stability, its endurance, and what
it has created that did not exist before—than to emphasize its origins."[14] There is much to be said in favor of making ego psychology
more central to psychoanalysis than perhaps Freud himself did.
Still, it would be wrong to jump from the banal fact that "from infancy to adulthood is a long time"[15] to the conclusion that Freud's
emphasis on genetic explanations, instinctual origins, and infancy
was exaggerated. In place of what Ricoeur calls Freud's archaeology, the revisionist emphasis on the ego's independence
from the id offers only a return to the myth of the autonomous individual. We are asked to forget all that Freud has taught us about
thick human conditioning, about how the unconscious ensures
that the infantile is always our contemporary.

To do justice to the complexity of Freud's account, it is
necessary to pursue the interplay between new and old in our mental lives hinted at by sublimation but never developed.* In terms
of this interplay, the difference between repression and sublimation is no longer merely quantitative. Repression is centrally the
repression of *ideas;* it must be understood as a corruption of *meaning* as well as a damming of energy. That is to say, repression tells a
story about an unconscious which is nevertheless fully continuous
with consciousness in containing purposive mental processes. To
understand the unconscious is to know the motives, not just the
mechanics behind repression. Thus, Freud's *Papers on Metapsy-*

*The following account follows the work of Ricoeur in *Freud and Philosophy:
An Essay on Interpretation,* tr. D. Savage, 170–176, 483–493.

chology make the relation to consciousness definitional of repression: repression protects the ego by hiding from consciousness ideas representing instinctual impulses. These ideas, we have seen, become fixated in the unconscious, cut off from sharing in future mental development, archaic survivors seeking disguised expression in forms tolerable to the repressing agent. But the expression, when it occurs, is no longer decipherable to the skewed self-understanding of the host self; repression cuts mind off from ability to reflect upon much of its own content.

Because the crucial work of repression is its skewing of self-understanding, its undoing requires *psychoanalysis:* an attempt to decipher on the level of meaning the censored text of the unconscious. This kind of analysis of meaning would hardly be called for if, as Freud sometimes assumes, repression owed its importance simply to the blocking of a certain *quantum* of instinctual energy. Therapy for such blockages could take purely technical forms and would not require the active participation of the patient. The fact that the mature Freud is a stranger to such treatments indicates that repression must be placed within a history of consciousness as well as within what Ricoeur calls an "energy economics." [16] Repression tells a story about a mind that is not a mere object governed by automatic principles of physics, but also a subject conscious of the meaning of its own experience.

By contrast to repression, the "way out" promised by sublimation is the way *into* consciousness: sublimation is that form of instinctual control which opens mind up to conscious acknowledgment of the whole of its own contents—down to the primal psychical representatives of bodily urges. Sublimation suggests the progress open to a self enabled to read the text of its own desires free from the corruption of repression.

In Ricoeur's terms, the sublimated self-understanding would seek to combine a regressive with a progressive movement. On the regressive side, the sublimating self would understand that its life was embedded in a never-ending process of desire, and that within every new activity were contained and renewed the unchanged economic tasks presented by the first mental representatives of the instincts. But unlike the fixated mental development attributable to repression, sublimation would allow for progress in self-understanding, the reworking of the primal "economic" tasks of desire on new stages.

An excellent example of this interplay of old and new within sublimation is Freud's well-known analysis of the *"fort-da"* game played by a one-and-a-half-year-old child.[17] The "only use" this child made of its toys, it would seem, was to throw them out of sight under a bed or table, to the pronouncement that the toy was now *"fort"* ("gone"). At first this was the whole game, but gradually there was added a sequel of retrieval; the child would repeatedly lower out of sight a wooden reel on a string and then yank it up again, to the chant of *"fort . . . da"* ("there").

Freud connects the purpose of the play to the child's cultural progress in dealing with the appearance and disappearance of the mother during the day. The game compensates for the pain of separation by expressing, on the one hand, defiant revenge ("All right, then, go away! I don't need you") and, on the other hand, a desire to master the situation, exchanging a passive and powerless position vis-à-vis the mother's leaving for a playful disappearance and return under one's own control.[18]

In *Beyond the Pleasure Principle* Freud attends to the striking way in which the child's game is but a disguised repetition of the painful departure of the mother. Why does the child have a compulsion to repeat and rehearse the unpleasurable experience? Freud first interprets the repetition as having an "economic motive"—the cathartic discharge of the tensions brought about by distress. But, as *Beyond the Pleasure Principle* is devoted to showing, the pleasure the child achieves by this kind of "play" is at a far remove from the commonsense understanding of pleasure. Against the outsider's view of the joyful child playing, *just* playing, Freud makes us see in the staged pleasure of infantile play an early example of sublimation and culture, a "substitute gratification" crafted by this child of one and a half years to compensate for the renunciation he made in allowing his mother to go away without protesting. This renunciation, Freud remarks, is "the child's great cultural achievement."[19] But it is a painful accomplishment and one for which the child seeks compensation in the controlled staging of exits and entrances.

Childhood play is thus the first in a long line of ambiguous cultural sublimations. On the one hand, the child has achieved mastery over the pain of absence by controlling its occurrence. In his "art" the child at play has reproduced and corrected the pain of reality. He has, in some manner of speaking, progressed by reworking his desires in a fictional setting. On the other hand, Freud himself emphasized the compulsive, even pathological aspects of the "*fort-da*" game when he called it a "repetition compulsion" and when he treated it as empirical evidence for the existence of the death instinct, of the yield of pleasure that comes from dwelling on painful memories.

One day when the mother returned after several hours, she was greeted with a changed game, the child now making itself appear in a mirror and then disappear to the chant "Baby gone." This expansion in the games of appearance and disappearance—peek-a-boo, hide and seek, and so on—is a regular feature of childhood. And the recurring theme of lost and found in these games puts us on notice that the need to master the anxiety of separation and the fear of absence stand behind the child's "playfulness." There is a structure to play as an early piece of sublimation that is hardly innocent of pain. The child at play is already a troubled child at work creating the two faces of sublimation: activity that compensates and substitutes for lost instinctual gratifications but only by painful acquiescence to separation and longing.

Freud's most sustained analysis of the duality of sublimation comes in his speculative reconstruction of the childhood influences on the art and science of Leonardo da Vinci. Indeed, Leonardo provides somewhat of a test case of sublimation. For if entrance into the sublime world of artistic creation and scientific research provided a progressive way out from repression for anyone, we should expect it would have done so for this consummate genius of art and science. To a certain extent, Leonardo's life did express the heroics of sublimation. While contemporary accounts suggest that he was almost an asexual human being,

> [i]n reality, Leonardo was not devoid of passion. . . . He had merely converted his passion into a thirst for knowledge; he then applied himself to investigation with the persistence, constancy, and penetration which is derived from passion, and at the climax of intellectual labour, when knowledge had been won, he allowed the long restrained affect to break loose and to flow away freely. . . .[20]

Alongside Leonardo the passionately engaged scientist, however, was Leonardo the obsessive, brooding artist, unable in particular to finish so many of his paintings. Contemporary accounts testify to the halting manner in which Leonardo's studio work proceeded—as does the slow death stalking the *Last Supper* in the twentieth century.

Why does Leonardo's life present this picture of contraries?

How was it that this unsurpassed portrayer of feminine beauty was so abstinent in personal life, writing in his journal, "The act of procreation . . . is so disgusting that mankind would soon die out if it were not an old-established custom"?[21] Freud answers by distinguishing Leonardo from the legendary Faust. Faust transformed the "instinct to investigate back into an enjoyment of life"; Leonardo did not.[22] "[H]e did not love and hate, but asked himself about the origin and significance of what he was to love or hate."[23] Leonardo, Freud reiterates, "investigated instead of loving. And that is perhaps why Leonardo's life was so much poorer in love than that of other . . . men. . . . The . . . passions in which other men have enjoyed their richest experience, appear not to have touched him."[24]

As if this were not sufficient, Freud criticizes the sublimated investigations of Leonardo for taking "the place of acting and creating." The scientific study of the workings of the universe imbued him with humility and awe, but it made him forget that "the way is open for him to try to alter a small portion of . . . the world."[25] Such passages attest to Freud's view that sublimation was hardly a "way out" from repression for Leonardo. Instead, "sublimation of the libido into the instinct for research [was] already a betrayal of Eros."[26] Leonardo may embody much that we admire in the scientific temperament. In an age of religion, for instance, he had the ability to face the reality principle sans illusions and consolations; but his reality was empty of love even as it was empty of illusion.

Having isolated the failures of Leonardo and traced them back "to . . . inhibitions in Leonardo's sexual life and in his artistic activity," Freud then warns us that it is no part of his purpose to turn Leonardo into "a neurotic or a 'nerve case,' as the awkward phrase goes."[27] Freud is well aware that, if artistic sublimation resembles neurosis in its construction of a world of fantasy, art finally distinguishes itself by returning to reality through its "artisanal" quality, its reworking of one person's fantasies into a public form of communication. And although this "art work" still bears a definite resemblance to the dream work Freud had analyzed in *The Interpretation of Dreams* (sharing the techniques of condensation, displacement, projection, and the like), there remains the difference that the concept of sublimation proposes to explain. Dreams and neurotic symptoms may "speak" the language of the unconscious—in technical terms, they may allow the mind to regress to the "primary processes" of the unconscious. But they speak only in order to disguise. By contrast, the work of art progresses forward into a lasting, public communication: it bestows conscious and objective form on the hidden content of the "primary processes" in a way that opens up new self-understandings for the artist as well as others.[28]

What Ricoeur calls the progressive and public aspect of art is evident in Freud's *Leonardo,* even though Freud's explicit procedure is to explain the meaning of Leonardo's paintings regressively—to see them as the disguised expression of one person's past. Freud explains the force of the famous Mona Lisa smile, for instance, as follows. A chance meeting with the Lady Giaconda "awoke something in [Leonardo] which had . . . lain dormant in his mind—probably an old memory . . . of sufficient importance for him never to get free of it when it had once been aroused."[29] The memory, Freud speculates, is of his mother. For the distinguishing feature of Leonardo's childhood is that it was divided between two homes. His earliest years were spent with his natural, unwed mother, but he was eventually summoned away from his mother to take up residence in his father's house. Giaconda's smile reawakened Leonardo's "long repressed maternal love," and he "strove to reproduce the smile with his brush." Smiling women appear frequently in Leonardo's paintings after the *Mona Lisa;* they "are nothing other than repetitions of his mother . . . , and we begin to suspect the possibility that it was his mother who possessed the mysterious smile—the smile that he had lost. . . ."[30]

Thus far Leonardo's act of taking up brush and painting the Mona Lisa smile seems similar to the wish fulfillments upon which dreams depend: an unreal, hallucinatory fulfillment of the child's desire to be loved by the mother. If one takes Freud literally, it is as if Leonardo has not created Mona Lisa, but simply, as Ricoeur puts it, "symbolized" the absence of his mother. But in the crucial paragraph in which Freud describes the glorification of motherhood in Leonardo's paintings, Freud adds this telling remark:

> It is possible that in these figures Leonardo has denied the unhappiness of his erotic life and has triumphed over it in his art, by representing the wishes of the boy, infatuated with his mother, as fulfilled. . . .[31]

The language of this sentence rewards careful scrutiny, as again Ricoeur has shown. Here, the "representation" that fulfills the boy's wishes is no longer described wholly in regressive terms—an abortive repetition of the childhood infatuation. Instead the artistic representation allows Leonardo to "deny" the unhappiness of his erotic life, to "triumph over" it in his art, an art that does not hallucinate an absent mother, but creates a present one and offers it "for the first time . . . to the contemplation of men."[32] And, in the four hundred years since that smile has been a presence within culture, not a fantasy, it has changed the consciousness of human beauty of all who have gazed upon it.

Taken as a whole, *Leonardo* suggests Freud's ambiguous attitude toward sublimation—toward culture in general and art in particular. Freud could write that the "artist has not far to go to become neurotic" outright: "like any other unsatisfied man, he turns away from reality and transfers all his interest . . . to the . . . life of phantasy. . . ."[33] But compared with the unqualified hostility Freud heaps upon the religious life of illusion and fantasy, he betrays a deep and abiding respect for art's "great refusal" of reality. In his analysis of the novelist Jensen's *Gravida,* for instance, Freud wrote that Jensen "directs his attention to the unconscious in his own psyche, is alive to its possibilities of development and grants them artistic expression." Art, that is to say, is similar to the act of psychoanalysis itself, insofar as each seeks to make "the unconscious conscious."[34] Each is an attempt to arrive at a language for making public the contents of the private mind. Each leads to progress in the struggle to heal the divided self, to win back from the reality principle more than a minor reservation for the play of the pleasure principle. This is why, on his seventieth birthday, Freud could attest to his alliance with the poets.[35]

But art finally does not put the truth first—in this sense it is more like religion than science, committed to the perpetuation of pleasurable illusions. To allow the conscious mind to confront the unadorned id—that was to be the task of psychoanalysis alone.

II

Plato or Freud on sublimation? As we have seen, Freud's sense that psychoanalysis uses the term "sexuality" in the same wider sense as the "Eros of the divine Plato" is flawed.[36] What Freud saw as akin in Plato is clear enough: the *Symposium's* narration of the human erotic journey from brute sexual attractions toward more sublime forms of procreativity and affection. But the differences obscured by Freud are equally important. In the *Symposium* Socrates is verbally initiated by Diotima into an act of love which is an act of "deliverance from the merely sensual." Love may begin by orienting us toward beautiful bodies, but Socrates' interest in these bodies is temporary, "only as steps" on a ladder leading from love of one beautiful body, through the love of beauty in all bodies, to the love of beauty in the inward rather than outer form, to love of the beauty of laws, institutions, and science, and finally to love of the Idea of Beauty itself.

To him who has ascended such a ladder, the "violent love of the one" with which he started now seems but a "personal trifle." It may be true that he has elevated himself to the higher mysteries of love by "sublimating" rather than "repressing" his physical loves outright. But the *Symposium* still concludes with the divorce of the lower from the higher, those who are pregnant in the body alone and those who create with the soul. At the bottom of the ladder, love is tied down to the cycle of birth and death. Procreation is a futile attempt to escape that cycle because *qua* desire, its creativity (procreativity) is itself part of the world of coming and going. A lover of this sort for Plato lacks personal beauty and strives after it in others to undo his own poverty and deformity. But not knowing what beauty is, in and of itself, he settles for possessing bodies and things whose share in beauty will inevitably fade. Such possessive eroticism reminds one of Freud's object-love, and, as pointed out earlier, the *Symposium* is consistent with Freud's emphasis on the impoverishment of the ego given over wholly to such a possessive stance vis-à-vis others.

At the top of the ladder, Platonic Eros has changed its nature in a way Freud disallowed. Man evolves from a desiring into a contemplative animal, and Eros completes itself no longer by appropriating objects, but by "knowing" at last the essence of beauty. "This, my dear Socrates . . . , is that life above all others which man should live, in the contemplation of beauty absolute . . . , the true beauty, the divine beauty, I mean pure and clear and unalloyed, not clogged with the pollutions of mortality and all the colors and vanities of human life. . . ."[37] Thus the *Symposium* ends with a transcendent image of love which does not contain and continue the physical, human sort of love with which it started, but which, having climbed the ladder, kicks it down. The *Symposium* ends with a very non-Freudian image of a human life beyond desire, at home in pure contemplation.

Man in Plato thus belongs to two realms—the sensible and the intelligible, the reality principle as it appears (and disappears) to our senses, and the absolute, unchanging reality of the world of Ideas, or Forms. But Plato's dualism is not yet the Christian gulf between man and God. In the Christian notion of *agape*, fellowship with God depends entirely on God's freely given gift of love, a love we do not earn. (Thus the King James Bible translation of *agape* is "charity.") There is nothing man can do by himself to bridge the gap between heaven and earth, to make himself worthy of God's love. God's gift of love is unmotivated by *our* value and is given to sinner and wise man alike.[38] From such a point of view, Platonic Eros seems impossibly egocentric and acquisitive. The lover knows only that he wants to possess for himself that which will make him *happy*. But in Plato's conception, this striving for happiness or well-being (*eudaimonia*) inevitably involves an ethical quest as well: "All men always desire their own good"; they "know that the happy are made happy by the acquisition of good things."[39] Their erotic acquisitiveness, crude as it is, awakens in them an ethical consciousness and concern for what are the really good things to possess, what is genuinely of value.

What the good is in and of itself the erotic consciousness does not yet know. But erotic consciousness is not akin to total ignorance either. The difference is that the ignorant self, "who is neither good nor wise is nevertheless satisfied with himself: he has no desire for that of which he feels no want."[40] But erotic consciousness, Diotima tells Socrates, is precisely this feeling of want, this aliveness to desire, this consciousness of imperfection and incompleteness. Here Plato and Freud are momentarily at one in insisting that desire is basic to the human condition. Plato sees this when he stresses the continuity between the lover and the philosopher. The philosophical temperament is marked by the special yearning for knowledge present in those who appreciate how much they do not know. Similarly, Platonic love is the awareness that the good and the beautiful are absent from one's life and the enthusiasm for finding them.

But there remains this crucial difference between Plato and Freud. For Plato, the ethical principle is included within the desiring self and thus Freud's sense of the irrevocable negation of desire by externally imposed moral authority is absent. Platonic Eros can freely develop on its own, given hospitable surroundings, into an ethical relation to persons and institutions. Freud, we have seen, could never quite develop such a doctrine of sublimation because the gulf between infantile desire and moral authority is absolute—the superego arises from without, an authoritarian structure imposed upon an always untransformed id. Precisely because Plato sees Eros developing by nature according to an immanent moral plan, Diotima can portray to Socrates the stages in that development as follows.

In its energetic striving for perfection, the erotic consciousness first takes the form of sexual attraction, stirred by the image of another's beauty. But even on this level, within the self's most basic natural impulses, a reaching beyond the self narrowly understood is implied by the desire to procreate. Through sexuality, we participate in the miracle of creation; we give birth in order to share in something that will survive our own death. Thus it is that the *Symposium* sees the most instinctual level of behavior as already containing the seeds of the most ideal level of behavior—the striving for immortality.

Since the desire for immortality is contained within sexual desire, Eros by its own accord progresses beyond the merely physical community of man and woman begetting children; the power of physical beauty may start the process of attracting one person to another, but physical beauty is not the *telos,* the goal and hence the true nature of such a process. What we truly desire to possess is happiness, well-being—the things that can be called good precisely because they fulfill our nature. To know *what* are these truly good things to possess becomes a human urgency. The mere possession of things good only by reputation or appearance no longer satisfies us. We strive to grasp the inherent qualities which make someone or something good. And we seek to transform ourselves in the image of the good we so find in other persons or things. This is the journey of Eros.

For all its mistrust of the body, the *Symposium* thus does give us a coherent image of sublimation by presenting a theory of human nature in which the source of moral judgment about the good is immanent to and harmonious with the pursuits of Eros after happiness.

By contrast, sublimation theory is Freud's great nemesis. His views on the "cruelty" of conscience led him to reject the reigning Kantian ethic and its setting of will over instinct, duty over desire. Such an ethic tends to instill ideals in persons without at the same time giving them a capacity to sublimate their desire toward these ideals. This is the scenario for neurosis:

> It is precisely in neurotics that we find the highest differences of poten-
> tial between the development of their ego-ideal and the amount of
> sublimation. . . . As we have learnt, the formation of an ideal
> heightens the demands of the ego and is the most powerful factor
> favoring repression. . . .[41]

In this way Freud is led to his famous endorsement of sublimation
as a "way out" from repression—an alternative ethic to what
Ricoeur calls the "violent shortcut" to instinctual control won
through identification with the parents. Sublimation replaces
identification with a slower process of *conscious* transformation of
the aims and objects of our desires themselves.

But Freud could not take his own way out. Dissenting from
Plato's hierarchy of pleasures, Freud insists that the economic task
set by life in a body can never be transcended; the "lower" instinctual and infantile impulses are continuously represented and reworked even within the aesthetic and scientific heights reached by
a Leonardo. And if the "loss" that comes from depriving an instinct of direct satisfaction "is not compensated for economically,
one can be certain that serious disorders will ensue."[42]

Because sublimation shares with repression a desexualization of
human interests, its ability to hold off the disorders of neurosis is
unstable. However "conspicuous [a] feature of cultural development," sublimation can sponsor only "finer and higher" pleasures whose intensity from the economic point of view is "mild as
compared with that derived from the sating of crude and primary instinctual impulses. . . ."[43] In short, the compensation is
precarious.

This problem with sublimation leads to grave difficulties for
readers such as Marcuse who wish to affirm the "self-sublimating"
trend within sexuality as a basis for a new and nonrepressive social
order. To his credit Marcuse faced up to these difficulties and conceded that if sublimation were to become qualitatively different
from repression, it would have to be "sublimation without desexualization."[44] But Marcuse's vision of such "nonrepressive sublimation" is befuddling. He is constrained to admit the obvious,
that the new, nonrepressive work and social relations to which he
gestures will not be "sexual" in the bodily sense of the term, and
that their eroticism will consist instead of sexuality "by its own
dynamic" transforming itself into gratification through "highly
civilized," "lasting," and "orderly" relations of work and love.
Marcuse has a great many terms to describe this uncoerced meta-

morphosis of "sexuality" into "Eros": "self-sublimation," "libidinal rationality," "the eroticization of the entire personality." It would seem that metaphor is being pushed to its limits here and that what Marcuse has in mind is a rather intellectualized version of Eros that even Freud would have had no trouble in liberating. To intellectualize Eros, however, is to end up with the same deflections, inhibitions, and desexualizations that Freud thought shaded sublimation back into repression. After all, Freud already appreciated that work

> is a source of special satisfaction if it is . . . freely chosen . . . if, that is to say, by means of sublimation, it makes possible the use of existing inclinations. . . .[45]

But Freud characteristically went on to qualify the affirmative potential of sublimation, to point out the limits and costs of Marcuse's self-sublimation (what other kind is there?) as a path to happiness. Not only did Freud think sublimation simply beyond the ken of a majority of persons; his deeper point is that even in the Leonardos among us, the ability of the sublimated lifestyle to pay its economic debt to the body is always in doubt. In terms such as the "eroticization of the entire personality," Marcuse stands in danger of obscuring the basic Freudian hesitancy over sublimation and returning us instead to an idealized concept of Eros not tied down to its bodily origins.

That some danger along these lines stalks his account Marcuse himself seems aware; he therefore calls his argument back with the vision of sublimation without desexualization:

> The instinct is not "deflected" from its aim; it is gratified in activities . . . that are not sexual in the sense of "organized" genital sexuality and yet are libidinal and erotic.[46]

But what could this language possibly mean? It is true that genitality does not exhaust sexuality in the body for Freud, but in what nongenital, bodily ways work or other general social relations could ever be "libidinal" and "erotic" Marcuse never sorts out. He is driven to speculate that "if work were accompanied by a reactivation of pregenital polymorphous eroticism, it would tend to become gratifying in itself."[47] This is increasingly bizarre. Workers cannot experience polymorphous sexuality in building a car any more than they could experience genital sexuality. The idea here is either ludicrous or a metaphor. And if a metaphor it is one that is distant from Freud's enduring insistence that sex is not (always) a metaphor. However much we—and Freud foremost—strive to accomplish the sublimations of passion to which Marcuse speaks, there is an irredeemably untransformed bodily dimension to pleasure that resists sublimation and qualifies the endorsement we can give it as a "way out."

The flaw in Marcuse's vision of Eros and civilization therefore is more theoretical than practical. It is not just that it would be difficult to accomplish what he has in mind; it is that the vision of Eros he offers is itself imbalanced in the direction of the sublime. It is one of the ironies of the vast critical literature on Marcuse's reading of Freud that the essential conservatism of his stance vis-à-vis sexuality has not been duly commented upon. Indeed the most remarkable feature of Marcuse's argument is that, in the tortured phraseology he has to employ to reconcile sexuality with "civilized," "orderly," and "lasting" relations, he ends up reinforcing Freud's own sense of the price we pay for culture.

By the time he came to write *One-Dimensional Man*, Marcuse apparently appreciated his own pessimism with Freud on the question of sexual liberation. He came to express his mood of resignation in one final tortured phrase—"repressive desublimation." Sometimes permission to have sex can be as repressive and dominating a form of social control as Victorian-style deprivation. This was Marcuse's lament for our own permissive society. If we are liberated to consume sex in the jeans we wear or the motion pictures we see, then sexuality loses its rebellious or countercultural stance and becomes instead the most powerful coin in which the permissive consumer society buys off the satisfactions of its members—even while containing them within domineering modes of work and social relations.

One is tempted to conclude, therefore, that Freud may have been right after all in his tragic view of civilization, since the "way out" from repression is so incomprehensible that we can hardly wrap our heads around the notion. But, although psychoanalytic theory reaches this pessimistic dead end with the concept of sublimation, psychoanalysis as therapy continues on with a project of personal liberation, holding out a promise of revised self-understandings beyond superego morality that will cleanse reason of its hostility to desire. It is to a discussion of psychoanalysis as therapy, therefore, that we must now turn, to a discussion of the possibilities for and limits to self-understanding Freud explored as a practicing analyst.

Chapter Seven

Therapy and Freedom

Freud allowed himself the rare optimism of believing that psycho-analysis would one day soon replace religion in the regulation of our moral lives. Civilization had gone as far as it could go with what Freud regarded as its infantile form of obedience to God the Father. With the end of religion in sight, the choice was between the regressive instinctual "letting go" that might follow the death of God or the long overdue emergence of the "rational operation of intellect."

Freud summarizes the project of rationality undertaken by analysis in his famous slogan, "Where id was, ego shall be." As with so much else in Freud, this simple line captures the dialectic between regression and progression for which psychoanalysis stands. The ego's hegemony over the id can only go forward if the ego dares to go backward to "where id was." And it is Freud's claim that at least with the guidance of the other, the psychoanalyst, the adult ego can finally regressively reawaken its long dormant infantile desires in a way that progressively ends the unconscious obsession with those desires. "[P]sychoanalytic treatment [is] no more than a prolongation of education for the purpose of overcoming the residues of childhood."[1]

Today, other forms of psychotherapy obscure the tension between regression and progression in Freud and would have us simply "live out," in Reich's term, suppressed desire. The contemporary form of treatment known as "primal scream" therapy carries this ethic of expressivism to its vulgar end in the notion that the repressed unconscious will cease to be repressed if it can be expressed loudly enough.

Freud's understanding of human liberation is once more distinguished by its sober sense of limits. The ego's visits to the id must take place under supervision; allowance for candid talk about sexuality must be strictly time-controlled. Above all else, Freud warned that instinctual freedom per se is no cure—for health or happiness. He knew that tracing neurosis to sexual repression would mislead persons into sexualizing the therapeutic process. Against no confusion did Freud issue more direct warnings than against this illusion that freedom inhered in easy sexual license:

> Ladies and Gentlemen, who has so seriously misinformed you? A recommendation to the patient to "live a full life" sexually could not possibly play a part in analytic therapy—if only because we ourselves have declared that an obstinate conflict is taking place in him between a libidinal impulse and sexual repression, between a sensual and an ascetic trend. This conflict would not be solved by our helping one of these trends to victory over its opponent. [2]

But then what does happen in therapy as the repression of instinct is lifted? What *does* it mean to say, "Where id was, ego shall be"?

Situated in Freud's own time, the psychoanalytic project of liberation did commence with the issue of sexuality. There would be no freedom until human ideals were brought into line with the animal truths of human nature. Against the dogmas of the priests, therapy therefore set to work on revising our self-understandings. The first step toward liberation was the seemingly backward one of "knowing thyself" by first knowing the body.

The radical reorientation of human ideals so as to accommodate the body would no doubt sponsor more space and tolerance for immediate sexual expression. The rational ego, Freud noted, will inevitably become "conciliatory towards the libido." [3] And, by contrast to the old order of repression and religious notions about sin and the flesh, Freud welcomed the coming sexual revolution as a long overdue victory for personal freedom and candor.

But the real task of liberation was to change our understanding and interpretations of sexuality, and not just to increase the mere quantity of sex consumed. Psychoanalysis teaches that a whole level of primitive infantile experience is beyond our conventional habits of self-reflection. So isolated from consciousness, the infantile desires have become fixated in their primitive form, achieving public expression only in unsatisfying disguises. Psychoanalysis further teaches that the essence of these repressed infantile desires is sexual. For this reason, self-knowledge of a wider sort requires us to pierce the disguises of culture, to reinterpret our seemingly civil, nonsexual interests in terms of their forgotten sexual origins. Without such a reinterpretation, childhood remains incomprehensible and self-deception continues to form the precarious base of civilized existence.

But the point of tracing civil interests back to sexual origins was hardly to advocate some belated liberation of the infantile. Therapy serves a different mission. By making the essence of primitive experience available to self-knowledge, we finally open it up to rational influence and molding. Therefore, it is the importance of sexuality to the work of self-understanding, and not just to immediate bodily expression, that explains the centrality of sexual enlightenment to therapy and liberation.

I

In the early years of his medical practice, Freud treated a class of patients whom he came to call "actual neurotics." Their symptoms were comprised of a chronic anxiety or apprehension directed toward no particular object or event and, as an aftermath to their anxiety, a general feeling of fatigue. In Freud's view, these symptoms were related to a sexual problem, but it was of the technical, not psychological kind: the effects of abstinence, frustrated excitement, or, as Freud puts it, unspent "somatic sexual excitation . . . transmuted into psychical excitation."[4] Since the problem was mechanical, the cure could be also:

> The necessary psychical relief can only be effected by what I shall describe as a *specific* or *adequate activity*. For the male sexual impulse this adequate activity consists in a complicated spinal reflex act resulting in the relief of the tension at these nerve-endings and in all the preparatory psychical processes necessary to induce this reflex.[5]

Freud never specifically abandoned the theory of actual neurosis, and one finds references even in the writings of his middle years to the "toxic" effect of sexual abstinence, to "nerve poisons" and to the need therefore to reform so-called civilized sexual morality in the direction of more actual sexual opportunity. Thus at one point or another in his career Freud pointed to the injurious effects of the moral ban against premarital sexuality; the inability of sex in marriage to compensate for its restraint before marriage; coitus reservatus as a method of birth control; sudden cessation of masturbation; and the taboo on so-called perverse sexual interests.[6]

But contemporaneously with his theory of actual neurosis, Freud put forth a fundamentally different, psychological account of the sexual denial which informs a "psychoneurosis." He worked out these ideas chiefly in regard to the symptoms of hysteria. That hysteria had something to do with sexuality was apparently known to the ancient Greeks, who named the disease for the behavior occasioned in a woman by a "wandering womb," or what we commonly today call a "hysterical pregnancy." The hysterics Freud treated around the turn of the century were likewise typically women, but their bodily symptoms duplicated not just pregnancy but a host of physical ailments from minor coughs to paralyzed limbs.

Freud, along with his early mentor and partner Josef Breuer, first approached the hysteric's symptoms in terms of a more general theory about psychic energy and its discharge. According to this theory, ideas and memories are not just expressions of meaning; they are also "cathected," or charged with a certain "sum of excitation" or "quota of affect." In the connections of normal thought process, the affect is properly associated in memory with a given event; thus to know the event cognitively is to react to it emotionally, to "blow off steam," to return the disturbed flow of psychic energy to its prior steady state ("abreaction").[7] But in hysterical connections of thought, Freud theorized that the connection between an idea and its affect had been broken and replaced with two puzzles. On the one hand, the hysteric may remember quite well a particular traumatic event, but she recalls it with indifference, as if it happened to someone else. On the other hand, the affect, or emotion, is expressed in some converted form—typically in the guise of some bodily illness afflicting the patient. To restore the affect to its rightful memory is therefore to facilitate the process of discharge, to allow the mental apparatus to have its delayed "abreaction" and dissolve the symptom. Catharsis is the cure, or as Breuer's famous first patient, Anna O., expressed it, talking is the cure. To tell Breuer openly what it was she was expressing in symptoms was invariably to dissolve the symptom immediately.[8]

However, Freud soon came to be dissatisfied by the view that catharsis alone was cure. Symptoms that had dissolved simply by being "talked out" reappeared in some altered form, and the process of discharge had to be instituted afresh. Freud recounts, for instance, his treatment of a woman who could not bring herself to nurse her newborn child. Hypnosis relieved the problem, but the next birth revived the difficulty and called for a new round of hypnosis.[9]

To move to a deeper study of symptom formation, Freud moved from studying the mind as a relatively passive apparatus for discharging buildups of mental energy to a more "dynamic" conception. In this view, certain ideas or events prove unbearable to a person's ego, which protects itself, as we saw in Chapter Six, by shutting the ideas out from consciousness, by repressing them into what we can then think of as "an unconscious." But what psychoanalysis means by an unconscious impulse is not to be confused with inactivity or passivity: the repressed ideas constantly seek return to consciousness, thereby requiring equally constant effort to maintain the protection which repression offers an ego. In Freud's view, symptoms are the compromised result of this dynamic conflict. They partly speak the language of the unconscious, and to hear that language is to know the primal ideas that spark a repression. But they are also a "substitute formation": the idea not as originally repressed, but as corrupted into an expression that consciousness can tolerate.[10]

In order to decipher neurosis as a language of the unconscious, Freud required a form of therapy that enlisted the patient as participant in a radical act of self-recollection. The suggestibility inherent in hypnosis as a form of treatment gave way, first, to a milder form of suggestive treatment in which Freud encouraged the patient to recollect the repressed memory (sometimes laying his hand on the forehead as if to help). Finally, Freud turned to the practice of free association, whereby a patient was encouraged to give spontaneous utterance to any thought floating through the head. This process, Freud thought, would avoid the opposing force holding in the repressed and would eventually shake loose the plaguing memory.[11]

In the course of practicing such a method, Freud found that patients' free associations almost always migrated into the area of sexual life and to sexual experiences they had indeed "forgotten" they ever had:

> unbearable ideas develop . . . chiefly in connection with sexual experiences and sensations, and the patients can recollect with the most satisfactory minuteness their efforts at defence—their resolution to "push the thing out," not to think of it, to suppress it.[12]

Freud put forward this notion that neurotics are defending against some kind of sexual secret gingerly at first ("I have merely to state that hitherto I have not discovered any other origin of it"), more forcefully over time ("I never find it otherwise"[13]), and finally as an absolute:

> I can only repeat over and over again . . . that sexuality is the key to the problem of . . . the neuroses in general. No one who disdains the key will ever be able to unlock the door.[14]

In his early writings, Freud is a literalist about the connection between sexual secret and neurotic symptom. An example of this literalism is his unraveling of a ritual performed by a woman in seating herself at a particular table, with a red ink stain on the surface, and in then calling in the maid to see her so stationed behind the stain. In analysis, it is revealed that the woman's husband had proved impotent on their wedding night, running to and from the room several times to make the attempt, and finally throwing a bottle of red ink on the sheets, exclaiming, "I should feel ashamed in front of the housemaid when she makes the bed."[15]

But here too the therapeutic effect of working through the literal, adult sexual conflict was short-lived, as if the most recent layer of trauma expressed in the ritual only masked earlier and deeper levels. The quick and dirty work of psychoanalysis as catharsis thus gave way to a longer, almost interminable process in which the meaning of the adult neurotic's behavior was traced back to certain core sexual conflicts of childhood. Freud came to see in neurotic symptoms secret testimony about the nature of early childhood, and it was by following this lead that he came to insist that to know what a neurotic is saying is to change our understanding of childhood and of sexuality as well.

Still, Freud's initial views on the hidden "sexuality" of childhood showed little of what was to come. In tune with common opinion, Freud still regarded children as asexual; the groundwork of neurosis lay in their seduction, or abuse, by elders:

The infantile traumas which analysis discovered . . . must without exception be described as grave sexual injuries; some of them were absolutely appalling. Most prominent among the people who were guilty of these abuses . . . were nurse-maids, governesses, or domestic servants, to whose care children are all too thoughtlessly abandoned. . . . [16]

At this point, therapy reached a crucial watershed on the other side of which lay psychoanalysis as we now know it. Freud could have stayed with the conventional assumption of children as asexual, taken the memories of abuse as factual, and turned in the direction of a radical, sociological critique of a seamy side of child abuse and development which certainly exists. But Freud was unwilling to credit totally the accuracy of his patients' recollections, given the frequency with which he was hearing the tale of seduction and the drift of his self-analysis into this same pattern. He therefore chose to continue the progress of analysis in and through the seduction memory itself, treating it as a fantasy but a fantasy whose sexual content requires us to comprehend childhood anew. This development gave to psychoanalysis a radical critique of culture far beyond what it could ever have achieved by merely pointing an accusing finger at individual child abusers. Henceforth, Freud's radicalism consisted in exploring the inevitable neurotic effects of culture on children, even apart from episodes of criminality.

Freud's repudiation of seduction theory has recently been termed a "loss of courage." This charge seems groundless, since Freud replaced seduction theory with the equally unpopular concept of infantile sexuality. More importantly, Freud never conspired to dismiss all accounts of infantile sexual abuse as the "lies of hysterical women." There remain in Freud's published writings several cases where he accepts the literal occurrence of some sort of assault or advance against children. In one case, Freud even sees through an adult's attempt to dismiss a young girl's accusations as fantasies. [17]

In abandoning seduction as *the* cause of neurosis, Freud did not hide the fact that real acts of violence occur against children. His point was only that infantile trauma over sexuality occurs in the absence of any assault, just as an assault can occur without triggering neurosis. To understand sexual trauma in a wider way, Freud thus turned to a study of infantile sexuality itself.

To lift the veil of ignorance imposed by infantile amnesia is to learn that the "sexual instinct" does not make its appearance full-blown at puberty, but has a developmental history commencing from soon after birth. Its aim is not unitary, genital, or reproductive and it achieves such an organization in most persons only after a painful and precarious odyssey away from an original bundle of component instincts capable of finding sexual excitability in every organ and crevice of skin. These component instincts are unruly to the highest, have no set aim or object, and include every manner of perversion and transgression, including those of sadism and masochism, in service to "the function of obtaining pleasure from zones of the body. . . ." [18] During this journey, libido flows through stages (oral, anal, and genital) which are predetermined and set by the evolutionary history of the species. But, however predetermined for the species as a whole, these sexual stages have to be lived through by an individual subject aware of its own circumstances and capable of reflecting upon them. These reflections inevitably surround the pull of biology with an inner life of fantasies, symbols, and memories not predictable in advance. Sexual development is therefore always precarious, in Freud's view, because the biological factors which move the component instincts toward integration in a heterosexual genital life are capable of giving way to mental fixations or inhibitions along the way. For reasons no theory can generalize, a life experience may cause one of the component instincts in the bundle of infantile body pleasures to fail to accompany the rest along the path of biological development; it stays behind as a permanent but unconscious fixation on an infantile gratification.

The central fork on this journey, the most difficult place to pass and the source of the greatest trauma, is the Oedipus complex and the instinctual renunciations it entails. Why the Oedipal trauma should constitute the decisive renunciation for Freud, more decisive than weaning, for instance, is not always clear, but it has to do with the cultural significance of this moment, the way it ends the history of sexuality in the family through the prohibition of incest and moves libido out into the larger cultural setting in search of satisfaction. Every "new arrival on this planet" is faced with the task of mastering the Oedipus complex and the taboo on incest:

> Respect for this barrier is essentially a cultural demand made by society. Society must defend itself against the danger that the interests which it needs for the establishment of higher social units may be swallowed up by the family; and for this reason, in the case of every individual, but in

particular of adolescent boys, it seeks by all possible means to loosen
their connection with their family—a connection which, in their childhood, is the only important one.[19]

The Oedipus complex is thus the essential destruction of the project of Eros within childhood, the creation of a cycle of desire which
requires other persons beyond the family for its fulfillment. But it
is at the same time "the nuclear complex" of a neurosis, a renunciation accompanied by feelings of guilt and remorse that are never
satisfactorily resolved, only reenacted. Since this is so, Freud can
conclude, we are all somewhat hysterical. We all suffer from the repression of our infantile lives. "[N]o qualitative distinction exists
between the conditions of health and those of neurosis. . . . [T]he
healthy have to contend with the same difficulties in controlling
the libido—only they succeed better in doing so."[20]

II

Convincing persons of the Oedipal foundations of mental conflict
proves no easy task. Freud refers frequently to the resistance provoked by a course of treatment so deeply wounding of the patient's
self-regard. The analyst must therefore be prepared to lay siege to
this resistance, forcing mind out of the dry and stable self-imagery
that is its best defense against regressive reacquaintance with its far
different origins.

But the destruction of resistance has its dangerous moment in
psychoanalytic therapy as well. There is a circularity to some of
Freud's case histories, insofar as the analyst justifies his interpretations precisely *because* they elicit the patient's emotional rejection.
This duality within resistance—the need to have the patient see
through the partiality of his own defensive self-understanding, on
the one hand, and the dangers in dismissing that self-understanding entirely, on the other—is best represented in Freud's most
famous recorded failure—the treatment of an eighteen-year-old
woman named Dora.

Dora comes to Freud suffering from chronic attacks of cough-
ing and hoarseness, low spirits, and occasional loss of consciousness. But she also comes with her own acknowledged "sharp-
sighted" and logical explanation of her problems. Her father is
having an affair with a woman whose husband ("Herr K.") in turn

is attracted to Dora. (It should be noted that Dora is fourteen when this peculiar love triangle begins to take shape.)[21] Dora has rejected her potential suitor's advances "with disgust," dwelled reproachfully on her father's complicitous attitude, become an openly hostile daughter, and developed her hysterical reaction.

One can, of course, readily imagine circumstances in which Dora's disgust at Herr K.'s advances would be perfectly rational. Certainly Dora's youth and the fact that her suitor was the husband of her father's mistress would have seemed to a mind less sure of itself than Freud's to be explanations enough of her disgust. But Freud's treatment of Dora is one vast attempt to destroy her confidence that her problems are as unambiguous as they appear on the surface. Perhaps, after the treatment is over, there will be good and nonneurotic reasons for Dora to spurn her suitor. But Dora's insistence that moral outrage is currently her exclusive feeling is belied by the hysterical symptoms she develops. This is Freud's warrant for insisting that Dora must have her neurotic reasons as well for spurning Herr K's advances. Not until these reasons are faced and acknowledged will Dora be genuinely free to say no for wholly rational reasons.

What, then, *is* Dora's sexual problem? Freud could not deny the truth of Dora's allegations about her father's intrigues, but he insists that Dora's literal reading of what is going on around her is nonetheless a misreading. In *her* case, literal-mindedness and moral reaction serve the purpose of defending against deeper truths. Satisfied that she has the "facts" right about others' sexuality, Dora can righteously avoid the study of her own remarkable turmoil over her father's intrigue. To study *that* subject matter, Freud tells her, would be to tell her own sexual secrets. During the course of the treatment, Freud takes aim at Dora's intellectual opposition by insisting that, for her, sexual repudiation spoke a deeper language of sexual attraction. Sometimes, Freud's combat slips into a petty kind of tyranny, as when he insists that Dora *must* let on to feeling *some* attraction to Herr K.—after all, Freud knew Herr K. to be quite a handsome man—or when Freud treats every denial uttered by Dora as a sign of resistance that circularly confirms the truth of his interpretations ("every no = yes").[22]

For the most part, however, Freud is after the more palatable point that Dora finds herself in an Oedipal situation where she cannot acknowledge the truth of her own emotions. However rational her sexual revulsion is on one level, she suffers her father's "wrongdoing" with the signs of jealousy and envy appropriate to a wife but not a daughter. It is this emotional, not to say hysterical, overreaction which she must face; she must find the illumination that will come from apprehending how implicated her sexual desires are in the doings of the father. In this regard, Freud seeks to convince Dora that her outwardly correct explanations (her father really is winking at Herr K.'s attentions to Dora) can be an enemy of self-knowledge; the very correctness of her logic prevents her from exploring the ways in which she is, of course, possessed of powerful sexual interests herself and is no mere moral adjudicator of the animal behavior of others. As the analysis proceeds, Freud seems intent on shocking Dora into how unbridled even *her* sexuality can be. Thus, she must feel some passion for as handsome a man as Herr K.; she really *is* acting like a woman in love with her father. Indeed, by the time the analysis is over, Dora has been told that she also harbors a strong lesbian attraction to the wife of Herr K.

Dora stopped her analysis after three months. She left as unfree and as unhappy as she came, still suffering from depression and hysterical symptoms. The analysis never moved beyond its backward-looking phase, never accomplished its admittedly destructive work of overcoming Dora's intellectual resistance to reacquaintance with the hidden dimensions of sexuality. Because the resistance could not be destroyed, the analysis was doomed to failure.

Of course, responsibility for the failure of her treatment does not rest with Dora alone. Freud's refusal to credit Dora's report that she felt nothing but disgust at Herr K's advances set the tone for the entire analysis. The message to Dora was that she could not be counted on to tell the truth about sexual matters, that she would resist the truth even when presented to her. In this way, Freud appallingly turned Dora's emphatic rejections of his interpretations into the only proof he needed of their truth. Dora's self-understanding was worthless.

In most cases, Freud remained more sensitive to the tension between tyranny and liberation implicit in his claim to understand persons better than they understood themselves. But the case of Dora shows that psychoanalysis quickly degenerates into petty tyranny when the analyst dispenses entirely with deference to the patient's own sense of her problems.

III

Ambivalence is the rule in analysis as in life elsewhere; alongside resistance, then, are the phenomenon of transference and the possibilities for radical influence opened up by the fatherly authority the therapist often gains over his patient:

> the patient sees in [his analyst] the return, the reincarnation, of some important figure out of his childhood or past, and consequently transfers on to him feelings and reactions which undoubtedly applied to this prototype.[23]

Freud was aware of transference from the time of Breuer's treatment of Anna O., the woman whose treatment Breuer broke off when she began to go into the throes of hysterical childbirth in his presence. On occasion, Freud recorded similar experiences, as when a "woman patient, whom I had repeatedly helped out of neurotic states by hypnosis, suddenly . . . threw her arms around my neck."[24] Unlike Breuer, however, Freud responded to such experiences by noting that "one could scarcely avoid, whether one wanted to or not, investigating the question of the nature and origin of one's authority in suggestive treatment."[25]

Freud accepted the reality of the charged feelings his patients directed at him. But he refused to attribute the provocation to any personal act or charisma of his own. Rather, authority inhered in the fatherly office he held. What was happening was that patients were repeating instead of remembering the past. For some, like Dora, this meant hostility; for others, like Anna O., it meant infatuation. In other words, therapy via transference was conjuring up a piece of real life.[26] The therapeutic transference itself was another edition of the old infantile conflict, an "artificial neurosis" in and of itself:

> In place of [the] patient's true illness there appears the artificially constructed transference illness, in place of the various unreal objects of his libido there appears a single, and once more imaginary, object in the person of the doctor.[27]

Freud understood the opportunity such a scenario offered him: to analyze the transference was to analyze the neurosis. With this insight, Freud abandoned hypnotism once and for all, the better to get the person's ambivalent feelings toward him out into the open. Therapy became centered on what happened in the session itself, on the analysis of the patient's relation to the authority of the doctor. And what Freud proposed to do, unlike authorities in other spheres of life, was to expose the irrationality on which his own authoritative appearance was based:

> the patient would like to behave in the same way as he did in the past, while we, by summoning up every available mental force [in the patient], compel him to come to a fresh decision.[28]

To defuse the authority invested in him as "His Majesty the Superego," Freud practiced one fundamental rule: total candidness. Anything can be said and everything must be said. No matter how unconventional or unpleasant or nonsensical the patient's thoughts, he must feel free to say whatever occurs to him. No one will mete out punishment or render moral judgment. Of course, Freud does not make himself the equal of the patient— only one person is doing this kind of candid conversation. But still this was to be an unusually liberal confrontation. This father wanted to know and to listen. The analytic session was to be a controlled period for verbalizing all that seemed most taboo about one's thoughts and desires.

Freud's patients seldom felt comfortable with the at-ease conversation he wanted from them. Whenever he touched on his attitude toward Freud, the young soldier known as the Rat Man could no longer lie still on the couch; he would flit rapidly around the room or cower in corners. It was as if, Freud suggests, the patient was protecting himself from the blows he expected in return for his confessional honesty.[29]

In the early days of psychoanalysis, while Breuer and Freud were still relying on hypnosis, the process of treatment was short: the hypnotized patient, with superego slumbering, was momentarily freed to experience unconscious desire. On waking, the experience proved cathartic enough to cleanse, at least temporarily, the patient of his or her more overt symptoms.

But cures easily obtained were retained only with difficulty. As we saw above in regard to the repetitive hypnotic sessions a mother needed to nurse each successive child, hypnotic cures had a short life.[30] To relieve symptoms without tackling the investigation of what those symptoms meant in the first place was to leave the substratum of future symptom formation untouched. "Hypnotic treatment leaves the patient inert and unchanged, and for that reason . . . unable to resist any fresh occasion for falling ill."[31]

Moreover, hypnosis glossed over the transference. Hypnosis

was just another version of hidden authority working its hocus-pocus, just a new dependency freeing no one. In fact, hypnosis was a form of cure that dramatically bypassed the patient's conscious participation altogether. If and when hypnosis worked, it did so by creating a submissive and suggestive state of mind in the patient—by placing the patient in a posture radically receptive to the doctor's suggestions. As Breuer's episode with Anna O. indicated, the hold granted the hypnotist over his patient could be strange and remarkable. The suggestibility of the patient bordered on love. Here, then, was the ambiguity inherent in hypnotic cure: it addicted as it cured. The old attitude toward parental authority was unknowingly transferred onto the doctor.

Freud was determined to devise a form of therapy that was immune to the charge of being but a species of suggestion. This is why the analysis of the transference held such importance to him. For instead of remaining an obscure authority motivating his patients through irrational emotion, Freud moved his authority out into the open. Freud made an *issue* of his authority itself.

All through his career, Freud was criticized for suggesting to his patients the dreams and memories psychoanalytic theory posited as universal. But what differentiates psychoanalysis from hypnosis and other manipulative forms of treatment is that, via the transference, the basis of the patient's gullibility is itself subject to analysis:

> In every other kind of suggestive treatment the transference is carefully preserved and left untouched; in analysis it is itself subjected to treatment and is dissected in all the shapes in which it appears.[32]

But if therapy does not work by suggestion, does it work by confession? More than once Freud heard from his critics that an analyst was nothing but "a secular father confessor."[33] After all, had not the church long known the cathartic effects of an oasis of honesty where parishioners could unburden themselves of their sins? This comparison slides over an extreme difference, well expressed by Freud. To the priest, one confesses what he conceals from others but knows himself. To the analyst, one must confess what he himself does not know. The catharsis that is immediate with a priest—or with a hypnotist—is a long unsudden process in analysis:

> He is to tell us not only what he can say intentionally and willingly, what will give him relief like a confession, but everything else as well

that his self-observation yields him, everything that comes into his head, even if it is *disagreeable* for him to say it, even if it seems *unimportant* or actually *nonsensical*.[34]

A species neither of suggestion nor confession, then, Freud's practice of therapy is well named "psychoanalysis." The appeal is to the liberating effects of *self*-knowledge. The person must comprehend for himself the repressed portions of his own life history. He must grasp the motives, and hence the meaning, of what has been repressed.

Of course, Freud understands the process of introspection in a unique way. Three points must be kept in mind. First, self-analysis will not do. Repression sets up hurdles in the mind which make a person stumble before the leap into the unconscious. Like Dora, a person must be forced, against the resistance, to look into what he or she has intentionally forgotten. Second, analysis places a premium on retrieving memory of early childhood—and on the assortment of dreams, errors, and mental lapses that Freud thought marked the way back to infantile experiences. In other words, what Freud would have his patients analyze is not necessarily what they on their own would regard as significant moments of their life worthy of so much attention. Third, Freud distinguishes between the active and passive arrival at self-knowledge. It will not do for the patient to be told about his unconscious. Freud believes the cure inheres in the patient's "working through" to his unconscious for himself. That is to say, it is as much the activity of confronting and breaking through the repressions that proves liberating as it is the particular pieces of knowledge picked up.

Little Hans, the four-year-old analyzed by his father due to a fear of horses (see Chapter Three), gave precocious recognition to the principles of analysis: if I *think* it, "it is good all the same, because you can write to the Professor [Freud]." Prior to the analysis, the four-year-old was unable to "think it good" to acknowledge his own Oedipal desires, let alone demand acknowledgment of them by others. The horse phobia, we recall, corresponded to a fearful coverup of Oedipal desire. The process of analysis for Hans was thus a process of coming into habits of self-reflection. But for this Hans needed another consciousness, that of his father-analyst. It was this analyst who first knew what Hans meant by his "horse nonsense." And it was the task of the analysis to deliver this truth to Hans.

The intriguing aspect of analysis is precisely this fact that self-awareness is sometimes an achievement brought about between two minds, rather than within one solipsistic entity introspecting on its own. Hans is liberated to recognize his own desires only with the help of one who knew Hans' desires better than Hans himself did. Thus we may speak of the liberating force psychoanalysis sees in self-understanding. But we must remember that psychoanalysis as therapy rests on the proposition that self-knowledge waits upon first being known to another. This "intersubjective" feature of therapy has important implications for politics. It suggests that self-understanding is completed only in communities of a certain sort—communities in which friends and fellow citizens, and not just professional analysts, know me well enough to help me know myself.

IV

Not everything Freud has to say can be reconciled with the description of therapy as a liberating self-reflection. On the other side of the ledger is Freud's well-known dismissal of free will as "psychic illusion." Determinism "in the psychical sphere," he writes, "is carried out without any gap." [35] And for psychoanalysis to allow a single breach in the principle of causality would already be "to throw overboard the whole *Weltanschauung* of science." [36] In the *Introductory Lectures,* Freud's most ambitious attempt at communicating psychoanalysis to the layman, he singles out the unreflective belief in free will for special whipping: "You nourish the illusion of there being such a thing as psychical freedom. I am sorry to say I disagree with you categorically over this." [37]

How, then, can we talk of therapy restoring to the neurotic ego the capacity for making autonomous choices if not even in its "normal" state does the mind have such a facility of deliberation? The problem we must face here is that there seems to be a contradiction between psychoanalysis as *therapy* and psychoanalysis as a *theory* of the mind. This is a point well made by Habermas. [38] In practice, Freud devised a technique of therapy in which the mind's peculiar ability to know itself directly, to mull over its own history, to rework the present meaning of past passages of life by reflecting upon them, is crucial. Time and again, Freud emphasized that there was no substitute for the subject's own active experiencing of his repressed unconscious. One could *tell* the patient what his repressed desires were. But not until the analyst's knowledge became the patient's knowledge did the information have enlightening effect.

Freud's practice of therapy, then, implicitly ruled out the efficacy of manipulating the patient from the outside—as if human minds were objects like any other objects, movable by electric shocks, chemical drugs, orgone boxes, or mineral baths. There remained an irreducible sense in which the human being must be approached as his own subject—as a participant in the constitution of his experiences.

But Freud's theoretical formulations on the structure of the mind—his denial of free will—are based on a different premise. Here Freud, like most of his contemporaries, held to the reigning positivist view that a science, in order to be a science, must issue forth in causal propositions. There was only one form of explanation, no matter what the occurrence to be explained, and that was to subsume an event under law-like propositions which specified the conditions necessary and sufficient for that event's occurrence. Not to offer causal laws was simply not to be contributing to scientific knowledge at all.

Freud rightly viewed psychoanalysis as extending explanation into realms of behavior previously dismissed as fortresses for the fortuitous and arbitrary: neurotic symptoms, for instance, or dream formation, or all those slips of tongue and pen we "normal" persons pass off without explaining every day.

Now it is one thing to find meaning and purpose in actions that previously seemed gratuitous. And Freud's great achievement certainly was to make such anomalies as dreams and neuroses meaningful to the person. But it is quite another matter to find such behavior not only *motivated* but *determined*. Freud's theoretical remarks on psychic determinism override the difference and speak as if an act without a cause is also an act without a purpose. Conversely, he speaks as if an intended act is also a caused act. Freud would have been closer to his own practice of therapy had he construed the compulsions emanating from the unconscious as being essentially different from the kind of causes which constrain events in the physical world.

It is in the analysis of those smallest slips of tongue and pen that Freud made his largest claims for psychic determinism; not even our errors are made mistakenly. Freud approaches the subject of mental lapses (the "psychopathology of everyday life") as if proof of causality here, in these trivial matters of no importance, would clinch the case in regard to larger decisions. For if the will is not free to make errors of its own choosing, where else should we expect to find its famed freedom?

In *The Psychopathology of Everyday Life*, Freud recounts the following error he was "forced" to make in the first edition of *The Interpretation of Dreams*. There Freud had referred to Hannibal's father as "Hasdrubal," when in fact Hasdrubal was Hannibal's brother. The father's name should have been "Hamilcar". Freud notes that "there must be few readers of my book who are better acquainted with the history of the house of Barca than its author"; how then did he come to overlook this error through three sets of proofs?

In the book, the error occurs in the context of Freud's relating the Hannibal fantasies of his school years and "my dissatisfaction with my father's behavior towards the 'enemies of our people'." [39] Freud had often given vent to this dissatisfaction during those years through another fantasy: "How different things would have been if I had been born the son not of my father but of my brother." (Freud's half brother, the child of his father's first marriage, was in fact old enough to be Freud's father.) "These suppressed phantasies falsified the text of my book at the place where I broke off the analysis, by forcing me to put the brother's name for the father's."

Arguably, Freud has taken an error which seemed unintentional and shown that its occurrence is packed with meaning, expressive of secret thoughts. One could readily agree with such an approach to the study of errors. But Freud wants to say much more than this. Not only can the error be interpreted after the fact; Freud maintains it was caused before the fact, by the unanalyzed compulsions of his unconscious.

The difference is illuminated by an exchange Freud had with a reader after the book was published. Among other examples, Freud had claimed that there was no such thing as picking a number randomly. Whatever number a person threw out, that precise number was determined by unconscious thought processes which analysis could reveal.

The reader suggested that Freud might mean something more minimal: the choice of number, in itself, is free and spontaneous, but once made, the number can serve to stimulate a complex pattern of associations which give the number its meaning after the fact.

Freud agreed that analyzing the meaning of the number was very much an association test, but he continued to imply to his correspondent that these associations were not merely reactions to the number; as unconscious thoughts they initiated the choice of that particular number in the first place.[40]

The *Psychopathology* is a vast collection of examples of such secret causal sequences in everyone's waking day. Whenever anyone forgets a name, substitutes one for another, or writes 1983 for 1984, or mislays the car keys or misses an appointment or knocks over an ink stand, the conscious may disavow the act, but the unconscious recognizes its determinations. In fact, in the Freudian schema, the unconscious simply is that hypothesis necessitated by the principle of universal intentionality. If all mental acts are motivated and some mental acts have no conscious motive, then there must be such a thing as unconscious motives.

The *Psychopathology* is a brilliant work; it is also the most popular book Freud ever wrote. Nonetheless, Freud may have misconstrued the nature of his own case vis-à-vis free will and causality. Habermas has adapted Hegel's terms, the "causality of fate" and the "causality of nature," to explain sympathetically the nature of Freud's misconception about the compulsions of mental experience.

In treating the body, doctors are presumably dealing with the causality of nature—with symptoms determined by invariable natural laws. Here one cures only by getting the causality of nature which brought on the disease to work now for the body. There is no idea of freedom from causation as far as the body goes. But in treating the mind, psychoanalysis grasps a different kind of compulsion altogether. Here the connection between symptom and infantile experience relied on by Freud is not rooted in invariable natural law, but "only in the spontaneously generated invariance of life history."[41] And analysis cures, not by working within the causal connection that is one's life history thus far, but by using the power of self-knowledge to dissolve the connection altogether, to reformulate the story of that life history. The body cannot, by knowing its subjection to the causality of nature, change that subjection. But the mind, by reflecting over its life history, can challenge the causality of fate. In this way, the *practice* of psychoanalysis lends its support, despite Freud's disclaimer, to notions of autonomy and free will.

We can now see that the only "freedom" against which the

Psychopathology argues is freedom considered as arbitrariness—
mere caprice or randomness. If what we mean by free will is such
anarchy, then Freud very much denies us freedom. A computer can
be programmed to spew forth words and numbers randomly, but a
mind cannot. Everything we do or say is symptomatic of who we
have become.

But this is no challenge to our freedom. Liberty does not disappear just because a person's life has taken on specific content. In
fact, the analysis of errors in the *Psychopathology* extends our sense
of control over acts we formerly were ready to disown as not of our
own making, as merely happening *to* us. Freud points us toward a
form of self-awareness in which our minds have become crammed
with *intentionality;* every act, from the most meager slip to the
most momentous of life's decisions, owes its origin to some purpose or motive of our own. Everything bears the imprint of our
purpose.

But has Freud further proven that these motives, purposes, and
intentions of ours are themselves part and parcel of an ongoing
causal process, perhaps ultimately reducible to quantitative propositions about the distribution of the libido? The premise of analytic
therapy is that the subject can at least suspend the causal process for
a spate; self-knowledge allows a person to see his own determinations clearly enough to be able to participate in the reformation of
character in a truly indeterminate way. Whatever he then does, it is
true that his every act will express, just as before, the new meanings
and desires he has chosen. But to say that an act is understandable
through the motives the subject attaches to them is not the same as
to say that motives are causes.

At the heart of the issue here is whether this peculiar ability of
human beings to do what stones cannot—to reflect back over a life
history, to mull and muse over past actions—makes any difference
in the way we must explain human behavior. Freud's emphasis on
the unity of causal explanation in science implies that the difference does not matter. Yet his practice of analysis remains one of
the great testimonies to the power of mind to know itself from the
inside, without the mediation of causal propositions.

As several scholars have pointed out, Freud approaches Hegel
through this testimony on behalf of the ''re-membering'' power of
self-reflection. What has been said of Hegel could be said also of
Freud:

The past is not just there for us to pick it up like an object. It is a creation, a composition in which the remains left to us are put into a symmetrical and self-educative whole.[42]

Of course, the self-education differs, Hegel's being a matter of education into the public texts left behind by our predecessors, Freud's a matter of private research into a personal past. As Ricoeur puts it, Freud teaches self-reflection via archaeology; the search for meaning requires one to unearth the archaic interests hidden beneath the mind's conscious contents. Hegel teaches the self-enlightenment of teleology, the self-understanding that we achieve by unpacking the future potential in past stages of thought.[43] Still, their histories of consciousness come together as the story of the gradual overcoming of self-deception by self-reflection. The mind remembers its past, and in remembering it, it "re-members" itself. To express the point in Freudian terms, what happens in therapy is that, through the act of interpretation, the ego comes to recognize the id as itself; the recognition leads to possibilities of "re-cognition" that change the meaning of the past for the future.

V

Freud saw himself as forcing his patients to be free by forcing them to be honest. Not until the resistance had been quashed and the repressed memories unveiled could the patient's introspections be trusted to tell the truth. Resistance, that is to say, kept persons dishonest with themselves as well as with others.

The end of the resistance was to be the end of the tyrannical phase of analysis. The future could not be interpreted like the past; as such it was beyond Freud's power to dictate. At one point in his treatment, the Rat Man asks Freud for a further guarantee about what will happen after he uncovered his repressed past. Freud gives him some general reassurances about the therapeutic effect of undoing repressions. But he does not—and cannot—tell him what attitude to take up toward his newfound desires, what laws he as his own authority should adopt to regulate the id. All such questions are beyond the pale of therapy, according to Freud. Therapy is *not* philosophy. Once the repressions are undone and the ego faces its own buried impulses, the future choices are exclusively the patient's to make. And because the patient can now make those choices rationally, on the basis of vivid introspection, he has the only kind of freedom Freud explicity recognizes: freedom as independence. It would seem a vital matter of principle with Freud that a therapist remain disinterested in the specifics of the value choices made by an autonomous will; therapy is to serve as no philosophy's handmaiden. Time and again, Freud inveighed against the would-be "psychological Socrates," warning that the positive instructions of a mentor do not readily complement the negative investigations of an analyst:

> Another temptation arises out of the educative function which in a psychoanalytic treatment falls to the physician without any special intention on his part. As the inhibitions in development are undone it inevitably happens that the physician finds himself in a position to point out new aims for the impulses which have been set free. It is but a natural ambition for him then to endeavor to make something specially excellent out of the person whose neurosis has cost so much labor, and to set up high aims for these impulses. But here again the physician should restrain himself. . . . [44]

In the free life, what instructs is simply the act of choosing for oneself. Honest subjectivity, Freud seems to think, is always honorable. He writes as if the old, enslaving imperatives were swept away as soon as the conscious form of reason replaced the unconscious form of repression. Philosophers from Plato through Kant have spoken similarly of the connection between freedom and reason. But these same philosophers also have spoken of the dangers of unsituated subjectivity. It is possible, after all, to free a person for evil as well as good. History has certainly seen its share of rational, even honest villains. Therefore, isolating "autonomy of the individual will" as the moral end in and of itself seems insufficient. One has to go on and specify some content for the will to will.

At times Freud is aware of this problem and disavows the claim that therapy contributes to a person's *moral* worth at all. Jones reports Freud's remark that "analysis makes for unity, but not necessarily for goodness." And a patient recalls being told that the therapeutic cure "simply means that a person gets on well: it doesn't mean that the person is particularly worthy. There are 'healthy' people who are not worth anything. . . ." [45]

Yet the general tone of Freud's remarks on therapy suggests he did believe analysis to be a kind of moral remedy as well. Like Nietzsche, Freud holds to an ethic of honesty: there is little worth to others in being grudgingly good. And, unlike Nietzsche but like Socrates in this regard, Freud writes as if no person who truly knows himself is capable of evil. "We tell ourselves," Freud writes,

> that anyone who has succeeded in educating himself to truth about himself is permanently defended against the danger of immorality, even though his standard of morality may differ in some respect from that which is customary in society.[46]

To understand why Freud puts such great store on the morality of the honest and autonomous will, it may help to refer briefly backward to his remarks against superego morality. It was Freud's view that our prolonged attempt to disavow the existence of sexual and aggressive desires has prohibited the development of a moral psychology among us. The disingenuousness of repression has claimed more than a few for criminality. For the lie of repression has the disadvantage of isolating our instinctual desires from the possibility of rational influence. The desires remain fixated in their infantile asociability; if ever the repressive controls fail, the resultant "return of the repressed" is not pretty. Honesty and self-awareness, on the other hand, by bringing the instincts into the stream of consciousness, defuse the power being generated by the repressive dams. They open up, for the first time, the possibility of the ego's recovering knowledge of the forbidden periods of its own life history. With such knowledge, Freud writes, reason is finally placed in a position to transform the instincts in a genuine moral act beyond mere imprisonment. Candor about the pull of the body is not a threat to morality, but its prerequisite. To quote Ricoeur, "There is . . . opened up a clearing of truthfulness, in which the lies of the ideals and idols are brought to light. . . . This truthfulness is undoubtedly not the whole of ethics but at least it is the threshold."[47]

There is a problem, though, with *Freud's* making such an argument on behalf of the new mediations of the honest ego. His "Copernican revolution of the soul" previously cast the ego as a virtual satellite of the instincts; how is it now possible for the analyzed ego to break loose and to exercise such free control over the id? Why is not the honesty analysis teaches only the candor to admit our total lack of free will? In answer, Freud cautions us against turning his remarks on the instincts into a "psychoanalytic *Weltanschauung*" of the id.[48] One must certainly acknowledge what has never been admitted readily before—the regressive pull of instinctual forces. But one must also recall that Freud has made the instincts famous for their plasticity as well as their permanence. Neurosis reveals the force of instinct in mental life, but it also shows the power of the ego to deflect the instincts into alternative modes of expression.

Analysis seizes on the truth implied by this conflict in the soul and enlarges the force of the ego by teaching it the "enlightened dictatorship of reason": the best strategy for moderating the desires is not to shut them out from the ego's organization, but to let them in.[49] An ego which recognizes the id as *it itself* is prepared to negotiate, to arrange a truce in the civil war. And by dispensing with the self-defeating tactics of repression, the rational ego eventually gains the upper hand over the id precisely because it accommodates the instincts. In terms of Freud's economics of energy, the threat of the soul bursting from unspent energy passes; the instincts grow malleable:

> all will be well if the ego is in possession of its whole organization and efficiency, if it has access to all parts of the id and can exercise its influence on them. For there is no natural opposition between ego and id; they belong together, and under healthy conditions cannot in practice be distinguished from each other.[50]

VI

Psychoanalysis provides powerful testimony to the liberating power of self-understanding. By extending the process of self-reflection into previously taboo matters of childhood and sexuality, Freud's patients were often able to interpret pieces of behavior—from dreams to neurotic symptoms—that hitherto seemed meaningless. Moreover, their interpretations illumined behavior in a way that changed character. The past was recollected in a way that altered its significance for the future.

Still, the self-understanding achieved in therapy was only partial. It was typically exhausted when directed toward the individual alone, as if identity were authentic only when the self was securely distant from others. Because of this lingering commitment to distance from others, Freud never systematically concerned himself with politics—and the liberating possibilities that a wider range of reflection about the self and its situation could yet hold out. He stopped with therapy and, in so stopping, acknowledged that psychoanalysis accomplished only a limited kind of liberation. Therapy emancipated persons from the dis-ease of neurosis only to return them to the dis-ease of culture. Therapy liberated persons only to return to what Freud candidly called "the common unhappiness" of everyday life.[51]

Eros, Friendship, and Citizenship

Freud's lament that therapy returns persons only to the "common unhappiness" of everyday life haunts all of psychoanalysis.

On occasion, Freud allowed that such common unhappiness should not exhaust our vision of liberation, that the civilization to which he was returning his patients was itself pathological, a communal neurosis. "[M]ay we not be justified in reaching the diagnosis that, under the influence of cultural urges, some civilizations, or some epochs of civilization—possibly the whole of mankind—have become 'neurotic'?"[1] With characteristic hesitancy, however, Freud refrains from affirming his own speculation. Viewed from the perspective of individual cases, a higher ideal of normality, beyond established social realities, remains irrelevant and inaccessible; the patient in therapy has little choice but to take social institutions as givens of reality. Or as Freud himself puts it,

> [i]n an individual neurosis we take as our starting-point the contrast that distinguishes the patient from his environment, which is assumed to be "normal."[2]

Nevertheless, as Freud's own quotations around "normal" above indicate, the assumption is unstable, and so is both the starting and end point of therapy. We are urged on in pursuit of a higher ideal of normality by Freud's own speculations about the communal neurosis:

> For a group all of whose members are affected by one and the same disorder no such background [of normality] could exist; it would have to be found elsewhere.[3]

To find it elsewhere, however, is to move from therapy to politics—from the negative work of distancing persons from the illusions of the past to the positive work of resituating ourselves amidst the attachments and allegiances that even for Freud characterize the distinction of human Eros. But Freud's science stops where value choice begins, and the most he could do for his patients, therefore, was to teach them the art of giving rational allegiance in place of infantile longing.

The refounding of moral and political conviction on the basis of rational allegiance to others cannot be gestured to with any easy optimism. Pre-psychoanalytic consciousness is not likely to fade entirely, and to that extent, communal identifications will continue to have the regressive appeal Freud elucidated in *Group Psychology*. But without blinking at the misuse of Eros in politics, no theory of human liberation is complete which leaves unillumined those aspects of character which develop only with the companionship of others. Outside of politics, friendship is the most recognizable example of the convergence of Eros, self-realization, and community. To reflect upon the Eros of friendship and the indispensability of friends to the enrichment of personal character is to gesture beyond the antagonisms of Eros Freud analyzes so tellingly. To see that citizenship aspires to be a kind of friendship is to keep the utopian vision of erotic politics alive.

I

The attachments and dependencies of friendship are commonly perceived as falling in between the intimacy available in marriage and family and the distance characterizing our relation to the political community. To some extent Freud followed this approach, mapping a continuum whereby culture deflects Eros from its sexual ties into increasingly "aim-inhibited" ties of affection. As a point along this continuum of cultural inhibition, friendships "are valuable . . . because they escape some of the limitations of genital love, as, for instance, its exclusiveness."[4] On the other hand, friendship creates a kind of exclusivity of its own, distinguishing out the very few from the general run of acquaintances and strangers. These few I can love, albeit in a sexually inhibited way, with a closeness reminiscent of kinship loyalty. Thus if any harm should come to the child of a friend, "the pain my friend would feel . . . would be my pain too—I should have to share it."[5]

Freud's choice of words here is suggestively intersubjective. It is not just that I feel for my friend and send him my sympathy. It is that I feel his pain as my own pain, that I keep his company in sorrow as in joy. Eros is quite capable of sponsoring such an attachment without direct sexual gratification, but only between a very few persons. What is beyond our erotic capacity is to universalize this sort of attachment, loving strangers as friends in the way Freud took the Christian notion of "love thine enemy" to demand.[6]

In our own culture, friendship's erotic side has become shadowy and metaphorical. The Greek term for friendship (*philia*) openly declared friends to be lovers of sorts. We typically speak of friends' liking (not loving) one another. Loving a person is one thing; liking is quite another, more moderate feeling, and this is the extent of passion we perceive friends as having for one another. Unlike the transformative love between child and parent, friendship seems a relatively distant phenomenon, a matter of wishing my friend well, as if I would not be around to participate in his well-being. I am happy *for* my friend whenever his aims and purposes find realization, but I can hardly be happy *with* him because those aims and purposes are his, not mine. I am not implicated in their existence in the sense of sharing them or participating in their definition, however much I can be of help to my friend in accomplishing them.

But sometimes our language and practice spy a richer, more erotic version of friendship than Freud's inhibited affection allows. Thus we speak of friendship not only as a special sort of interest between persons but also as a special sort of knowledge. And while any passing acquaintance can wish me well, only a friend can know me so well as to lay claim to participating in my well-being, by helping sort out the aims and purposes of a life in whose happiness his own has become implicated. This kind of cognitive competence and the deep, sharing version of friendship it makes available are hardly common. I am unlikely ever to meet more than a few persons who can know me at least as well as I know myself. But such deep friendship, in the midst of or apart from sexual love, is a recognizable experience only partly elucidated by psychoanalysis. When friends form a community in the above sense, there is a lowering of boundaries between selves similar to the interplay of pleasure between child and parent I discussed in Chapter One.

The absence of any sustained attention to friendship is symptomatic of Freud's tendency to approach human associations in terms of their power dimensions. In Freud's one book devoted specifically to the subject of group psychology, we have seen him tellingly limit his examples of common life to two—the church and the army. And his study of individual psychology is largely developed in regard to the superior-inferior relations of parent and child. I have argued that there is more to the infant-parent tie than a power relation, but there is no doubt that the generational difference makes for a relationship between unequals. As a relation between persons who typically understand themselves as equals, friendship is thus a fundamentally different form of association than those upon which Freud dwells, and its absence helps justify his pessimistic view about the hidden structure of human attachment.

As opposed to its unsystematic treatment in psychoanalysis, friendship becomes the highest virtue in Aristotle's discussion of the good life and the good city, arguably higher than even justice, because "when men are friends they have no need of justice, while when they are just, they need friendship as well."[7]

What Aristotle calls true or perfect friendship is wholly apart from Freud's submissive and possessive categories of love. There are imperfect forms of friendship which Freud's categories do adequately describe, as where the friend is loved only for the use to which he can be put or the pleasure he gives. Precisely because such friendships are examples of Freud's possessive "object-love," they are invariably flawed and fleeting—in retrospect hardly friendships at all. Freud's categories might also shed light on the imperfect friendship and affection Aristotle thought available within the family—marred in Aristotle's view by inequality between the generations *and* sexes.[8] But friendship perfects its nature only between felt equals, each capable of loving and being loved for who he or she is. This love is at once a form of self-love *and* altruism and hence collapses the antagonisms of psychoanalytic Eros. Friendship is altruistic in that to love a friend for who he is, rather than for his use, is to wish the good for him for his own sake. But altruism of this sort is not yet friendship; it can be felt and delivered from a distance and apart from the familiarity and keeping company that differentiates friends from universal ambassadors of good will. Friends, remarks Aristotle, are *demanding* about one another's company—they seek to constitute a life together, following and sharing in each other's pursuits and entering into the other's life as one of the good things about that life. To want the good for my friend therefore is to want the good for that which has become my own good:

> [I]n loving a friend men love what is good for themselves; for the good man in becoming a friend becomes a good to his friend. Each, then, both loves what is good for himself, and makes an equal return in good-will and in pleasantness. . . .[9]

Friendship thus is the most recognizable and perhaps most important good the self cannot have alone: "[E]ven those who are supremely happy desire to spend their days together; for solitude suits such people least of all."[10] But in the final analysis "people cannot live together if they . . . do not enjoy the same things. . . ."[11] That is to say, friends are companions in *shared* activities and undertakings, and it is this *common* life that makes friendship relevant to politics as an erotic experience that changes the respective selves who are friends.

II

From friendship to citizenship can be a very long way. In every city, Aristotle remarked, there seems to be a kind of friendship among citizens—"at least men address as friends their fellow voyagers and fellow soldiers, and so too those associated with them in any other kind of community."[12] But the "very characteristic of friendship" is living together and "it is a hard business for this condition to be fulfilled with a large number."[13] Citizenship's hold on Eros and on friendship, therefore, will always be partial, and this is one reason why concord in the city requires legal as well as erotic ties: treating according to the ways of justice even those with whom we are not personally familiar. But to find a city where citizens have no fellow feeling for one another at all is to find a collection of individuals which is a "city no longer."[14]

For Freud also, we have seen that Eros informs and holds together political community—but without the redeeming features of friendship. In *Group Psychology,* group members identify with one another only indirectly, through the mediation of their collective, overlapping love for the same father-leader. Such collectivized love makes community solid for Freud, but it has little or nothing to do with active, self-enriching participation with others in a common life. Instead, what Freud bleakly describes is the process of totalitarian deindividuation, whereby erotic identification with the fatherland strips the individual of his distinguishing conscience and reduces him to a piece of the undifferentiated, manipulated mass.

If the solidity of political community is invariably entwined with the creation of mass individuals, then one must in the end side with the stark antipolitics of *Group Psychology.* The ideal of erotic politics, so utopian-sounding, would but welcome totalitarianism. But *Group Psychology* gives an incomplete description of the erotic forms political community can assume. Freud makes *vertical* identifications between a mass of individuals, on the one hand, and a focal leader, on the other, the skeleton of all forms of politics, and he comes close to ridiculing democracies of the American sort for being eccentrically leaderless and culturally "impoverished."

Freud's disdain for "American ways" does have its polemical point: insofar as contemporary liberalism insists that political community should refrain from endorsing any particular, moral vision of the good life, it is difficult to experience one's *horizontal* relation to fellow citizens as a meaningful relation or as having any defining impact on one's own aims and purposes in life. We have become strangers and aliens all.

But political vision is not exhausted by Freud's choice between the erotic but tyrannical vitality of primal hordes and the psychological emptiness of "American ways." At its best, politics aspires to awaken the Eros of the political animal, through the experience of friendship, to the good "we can know . . . in common" that no one self could know alone. [15] Citizenship—involving loyalty to a common way of life—regains its enriching impact on the self to be realized.

Not every community, in fact very few, can lay claim to the kind of loyalty that transforms the member giving it. Not every social influence on a citizen's identity can maintain the hold of continued allegiance upon rational reflection. But communities

open to democratic participation and self-management can, at
their best, inspire just such rational allegiance. Citizens then find
constitutive elements of their own egos reflected in and shared by
others. They realize that they are engaged with these others in a
common undertaking to preserve and perfect a way of life without
which there would not be selves of their particular sort.[16] Indeed,
apart from such a common venture, the richer dimensions of personal character—the virtues of loyalty and solidarity, of friendship
and allegiance—could have only narrow and shadowy existence.

If we count it a virtue to have friends and to entertain special
loyalties and obligations to persons as friends, then liberation of
the atomized sort cannot be the finale for freedom. If personal
character is to be enobled by the capacity for loyalty and solidarity,
then free men and women must live in communities as friends and
citizens, and not always as strangers. Freedom depends on obligation as well as on liberation.

Conclusion: The Limits of Liberation

There are signs everywhere that the era of liberation in American culture is drawing to a close. Groups such as Moral Majority have popularized a lament for the lost purity of American life, seeing corruption where others have seen freedom. Moreover, in contrast to the future confidently assumed by Freud, religion appears ready to reassert a certain primacy over politics, replacing public policies premised on privacy and free choice (for instance, on issues such as school prayer or abortion) with a new set of state sanctified orthodoxies.

Set against the new vocabulary of politics and moral corruption, the ethic of liberation, as it has reshaped American culture over the last two decades, comes into focus. Its core ideal can be stated as follows. Society is composed of a plurality of persons, each with his or her own values, preferences, and aims in life. Each person's aspirations are entitled to equal social respect and there can, therefore, be no legislated orthodoxies about the truly good or right purposes to have in life. Instead, politics must remain neutral in the competition among conceptions of the good life, seeking only to permit the fullest possible expression of the plurality of persons we are.

I

This vision of liberation must be given its due. Its immediate impact was to usher new possibilities for political, artistic, and sexual expression into the stale world of 1950s conformity. In regard to sexual lifestyle in particular, what we commonly call "sexual liberation" accomplished a long overdue expansion in the realm of tolerance. To allow persons free choice when it comes to issues intimately touching the self testifies, after all, to our belief that there are no right answers to questions of sexual morality—only answers that reflect the irreducible differences among persons. Indeed, we prefer to speak of sexual lifestyle, rather than sexual morality. The former phrase captures our conviction that sex is fundamental to individual self-expression; as such it now inherits the tolerance we have long since bestowed upon religious or intellectual or artistic expressions of who we are.

However rich in these respects, the contemporary vision of liberation is still partial. The limits to liberation for which I have argued in this book are more theoretical than practical. It is not just that it proves difficult in practice to live up to the ideal of self-expression; it is that the ideal itself is flawed. In tune with Reich but not Freud, the self to be expressed is increasingly of the atomized and alienated sort. Such a self may achieve many commendable traits of character—autonomy of will, for instance, or tolerance and respect for others. Due to his rootless circumstance, however, the atomized self must be a stranger to the civic set of virtues which once completed the development of character—loyalty and solidarity, citizenship and public allegiance.

This may overstate the case a bit. Perhaps modern liberated men and women still practice the virtues of solidarity in the company of family or friends. But that is the outermost reach of our convictions of loyalty, of our experience of a common identity. Personal character is no longer implicated in any wider set of political arrangements; citizenship and civic consciousness have all but lost their relevance to persons' attempts to understand and express themselves. The consequence is an impoverishment in the range of virtues and qualities there are to express.

II

The limits to the contemporary ethic of liberation suggest limits to the vision of liberal political psychology as a whole. Hobbes, for instance, defined freedom as follows: "Liberty, or freedom, signifieth, properly, the absence of opposition; by opposition, I mean external impediments."[1]

According to Hobbes' account, I am apparently free so long as I can pursue without external restraint the objects of my desires. That I may not be able to choose what desires to have, that I am constrained by my nature as a human being to have characteristic needs, does not in the slightest prevent me from acting on the basis of *my* needs and *my* desires.

For Hobbes, I am also in privileged possession of knowledge about who I happen to be. Simply by being myself, I know transparently what it is I desire. Thus I become unfree only in the world of action, when someone or something outside myself prohibits me from acting on self-knowledge, from satisfying my known needs.

Hobbes thus set up the following well-known tension. Alone, apart from society, beyond the constraining influence of other persons, each of us is born free in a state of nature. But such freedom entails an indiscriminate letting loose of human desire that leaves life "nasty, mean, poor, brutish and short." Hobbes himself resolved this tension by devising a politics against liberation, a Leviathan that provided its citizens with security in return for obedience.

Although Leviathan gives way in the history of modern political thought to the minimum state, classical liberalism takes over intact Hobbes' psychology regarding the privilege of each individual to know and act on the basis of transparent self-knowledge. For liberals of the utilitarian persuasion (Bentham, for example), this is evident from the fact that the happiness they seek to maximize in society is simply the aggregate of the private preferences of individuals, each self knowing its own preferences through immediate introspection. For liberals of the contractarian tradition (Locke is an example), the subject of the social contract is likewise seen to be an individual whose interests are readily identifiable and knowable prior to the institution of society. In either the utilitarian or contract view, then, freedom revolves around social space for expressing this self we immediately know ourselves to be; the potential obstacles to such a process are comfortably external and social.

We have seen Freud cast doubt on such a path to liberation. Via the concept of the repressed unconscious, psychoanalysis calls into question the notion of self-transparency—introspection stymied only by distant obstacles. The Freudian concept of repression, for instance, includes more than just the crude notion that society frustrates sexual desire. Other animals can be frustrated, but only human beings can be repressed; the difference is that human beings alone internalize an ideal image of themselves (the superego) that henceforth sets them at odds with the first givens of nature (the id and its instincts). This point requires further consideration.

For Hobbes, man was both a rational and a desiring animal, but no tension was possible between these two realms of behavior. Reason could "scout" for, but never contradict, desire. Crucially, one's reason was preprogrammed to define the good life and the world of values always in terms of one's interests. Thus, for Hobbes, human behavior had an overarching, if biased, unity.

Repression is the psychoanalytic doctrine that fractures such unity, revealing that the human predicament is to have a nature unexhausted by so-called laws of nature or by the determinism of bare instinct. Human beings can raise themselves higher and degrade themselves lower than other animals precisely because who we are is not synonymous with the givens of nature, as Hobbes thought. We characteristically contradict ourselves, we make or remake our own identity in terms of ideals that do not necessarily serve or even answer to our instinctual self. By *reflecting* on who we are, we *interpret* who we are and in this way participate in the constitution of a self.

That self-knowledge can rework the import of past life history means we are potentially free in a way Hobbes rejected. (Our desires are not simply engraved in stone.) It also means that the Hobbesian understanding of liberation must be reworked in light of Freud. First, the crucial obstacles to my acting on my own desires have become part of myself, my superego. Second, doubt has been cast upon the underlying image of liberation itself. It seems Hobbes' vision ironically reduces freedom to a state of perfect obedience to the brute force of the laws of nature, to the accidental desires we happen to have.

Consider, then, the more recent and "psychological" version of liberation offered by Reich:

> It [is] necessary to distinguish natural needs for happiness from secondary asocial drives produced by compulsive education. Secondary, unnatural, asocial drives ... entail moralistic inhibition. However, the gratification of natural needs can be governed by the principle of freedom, by the principle of "living out" if you like.[2]

This "updated" version of liberation accepts the presence of obstacles to freedom within as well as without the person, and the need, therefore, for psychological change to accompany political reform. But Reich and the psychology that flows from his theories made the obstacles internal only in a superficial sense. The self is seen as thinly "conditioned" or "educated" into a new set of desires or beliefs that control a deeper and more "natural" order of desires. The conditioned set of beliefs is worn by the "true" self as a mere veneer or overlay. What is needed, therefore, is only to strip the self of this layer in order to return to the self underneath. Reich, not Freud, thus seems closer to the practice of the "permissive society."

The deficiency of the Reichian account is that it still shares with the Hobbesian version of liberation the assumption that the self to be liberated is unproblematic, available intact underneath the thin skin of conditioning. Liberation is still a simple matter of discovering the self, not creating one. The self remains conceptualized as a brute natural fact, an entity predefined by nature outside of society in accordance with innate needs and instincts. Precisely because this view of freedom identifies our "true selves" with fixed human nature, it can only identify the impact of society on the individual as superficial and harmful. Society's work is superficial because it can do no more than place an overlay on our unchanging nature; it is harmful in that this overlay restricts the underlying, more "natural" level of needs. Thus psychotherapy of the Reichian sort can only aggravate the tension between individual and society already present in the theories of Hobbes and Locke.

The difficulties with both the Hobbesian and Reichian accounts of liberation lead one to turn to the powerful alternative account of freedom that owes its origin to Kant. For Kant, Hobbes' so-called freedom from external obstacles still left the self radically dependent on and determined by causes and forces over which it had no control. It made little difference to the cause of freedom that these causal forces were internal, that they could be called "our nature." The fact remained that the self was left to obey laws of nature it did not choose. In no meaningful sense were persons the authors of their actions.

Kant concluded that if there was to be human freedom at all, it must be because we are able to transcend this level of causal action entirely. It must be because there is a self to be liberated from both nature *and* society, from determined and causal behavior rooted in obedience to instinct and from the determined behavior of our socially acquired character.

Kant pointed to the existence of such a self, albeit a bare one prior to both what nature implants and what society adds. This bare self he identified with pure reason. Kant's pure reason was more powerful than Hobbes' instrumental reason in that it could do more than slavishly serve as the instrument for achieving un-willed desires. Pure reason was the self's capacity to choose its own ends in life, to will goals and values via a rational process unaf-fected by accidental circumstances.

On the surface, Kant's project of liberation has its similarities to that offered by Reich. The crude psychotherapeutic project and the Kantian approach share the crucial belief that the self to be liberated must exist prior to its socially given content and ex-perience. In this sense, Reich and Kant are similar not only to each other but also to Hobbes. They distinguish themselves from Hobbes because now the project of liberation is complete only when this "true" or "prior" self is freed from even the internal-ized social dimension of character. Reich summarizes the indis-criminate sweep of his own project when he says that the enemy is character itself—"armor" acquired in society that weighs heavily on the natural self.

The profound difference between Reich and Kant is that Reich continues the search for this "natural" self of innately given, as opposed to socially given, desires. In contrast, Kant's "prior self" is a self prior to natural and social determinations alike. For Kant, the project of liberation is complete only when the self freely wills for itself unbiased by who one happens to be by *birth* or by *ex-perience*.

It is to Kant, then, that we must turn to understand what is wrong with paths of freedom that take one "back to nature," with projects of liberation that perceive liberty as a battle *for* nature *against* society. If what one means by freedom is wrapped up at all with notions of choosing for oneself, of taking responsibility for the contents of one's choices, then Kant is surely right that this project of autonomy does not side with nature against culture. Autonomy does, in a manner of speaking, side with reason rather than desire. For reason *is* the self's capacity for self-governance, its ability to freely frame the principles of right and wrong that guide behavior. Desire, on the other hand, is the capacity of the self to be determined by instinct and to be manipulated by social rewards and punishments.

Where does Freud stand? On the one hand, psychoanalysis as therapy is a carrying forward of the Kantian project of autonomy, the expansion of the control of reason over the hitherto unexplored continent of the unconscious. On the other hand, we have seen that Freud's dispute with Kant is quite large. The theory of repression is an attack on Kant's cruel and categorical divorce of duty and desire, is and ought, the empirical and the ideal. Pure reason does not make one free; for Freud, it leads to neurosis. Hobbes may have been too brutish in reducing reason to the status of servant to desire, but equally destructive is Kant's proposal to make reason and duty autonomous of desire. Such an ideal of autonomy is an attempt to live beyond our psychological means; it is an illusory ideal maintained only through the dirty work of repression. Moreover, the self freed is not the distinct self within whose bounds "I" live, as even Kant himself admitted. The particular desires of each person are instead replaced by the undifferentiated and unlocated status we share as rational beings.

Freud therefore warns of two mistaken projects of liberation. The first identifies ourselves too completely with instinctual expression, thereby confusing freedom with determinism and leaving unexplained the very fact of repression, that we are not harmonious with our desires, that we do strive to idealize our own nature. The second mistaken path identifies ourselves too purely with reason, thereby seeking to deny the constraints of nature that are not open to us to deny. A truer account of liberation thus waits on a reconciliation of reason and desire, a reconciliation which we have seen Freud gesture toward in his concept of sublimation and in his practice of therapy but which he does not complete.

Hobbes fashioned a politics *against* liberation because his image of human nature loosened proved too frightening. On this particular point, Freud is similar. If the only self to be liberated is the self of instincts and appetite, one must side with the forces of control. But finally Freud surpasses Hobbes by giving us a deeper account of the self to be liberated. This self is neither exhausted by nor identified with forces and drives operating in tune with laws of nature. If that were all the self amounted to, there would never have been any sense to psychoanalysis as *self-reflective* therapy. Of course, this is not to say one is totally free to make and remake oneself. The instincts exist and constrain—a point Freud makes repeatedly in "economic," or quantitative, terms. But my image of myself is powerful enough to participate in reconstituting the meaning of what otherwise would be a mere string of accidental life experiences, a mere concatenation of events befalling me.

One finds, therefore, in Freud's writings an account of the project of liberation available to the self when it struggles, against both social conditioning and natural determinants, to participate in creating its own identity. This is Freud's distinct contribution to the liberal vision of the autonomous ego—the freeing of the self from obstacles to self-realization, the dispossession of obsessive attachments to the past. "Where id was, ego shall be."

Freud the therapist offers his patients nothing beyond this act of dispossession—only resignation to the cold necessities of reality unadorned with illusions. Therapy can provide no answer to the desiring animal who reflects on what he ought to desire in life. But politics takes up where therapy leaves off. However substantial the achievement of autonomy through therapy, the self-knowledge of the analyzed self will always remain incomplete, limited to what one can know about the isolated individual. Such self-understanding cannot illumine, much less support, the richer civic aspects of personal character—the virtues of fellow-feeling and friendship, of citizenship and allegiance to a common good. These virtues are either realized through politics or not at all.

Notes

The following abbreviations refer to the editions of Sigmund Freud's work cited most frequently in the notes below:

SE = *The Standard Edition of the Complete Psychological Works of Sigmund Freud*, ed. James Strachey, in collaboration with Anna Freud, assisted by Alix Strachey and Alan Tyson (24 vols.). London: The Hogarth Press and the Institute of Psycho-Analysis, 1953–1966.

CP = *Collected Papers*, ed. James Strachey and Joan Riviere (5 vols.). London: The Hogarth Press and the Institute of Psycho-Analysis, 1957.

INTRODUCTION: *Two Notions of Freedom*

1. Herbert Marcuse, *Eros and Civilization: A Philosophical Inquiry into Freud* (New York: Vintage Books, 1962) and Philip Rieff, *Freud: The Mind of the Moralist* (New York: The Viking Press, 1959) and *The Triumph of the Therapeutic: Uses of Faith After Freud* (New York: Harper & Row, 1966). Other influential books on Freud's relation to moral and political philosophy include Norman O. Brown, *Life Against Death: The Psychoanalytic Meaning of History* (Middletown, Conn: Wesleyan University Press, 1970); Paul Ricoeur, *Freud and Philosophy: An Essay on Interpretation*, tr. D. Savage (New Haven: Yale University Press, 1970); Jurgen Habermas, *Knowledge and Human Interests* (Boston: Beacon Press, 1971); and Stan Draenos,

Freud's Odyssey: Psychoanalysis and the End of Metaphysics (New Haven: Yale University Press, 1982).

CHAPTER ONE: *Eros and Politics*

1. *An Outline of Psycho-Analysis,* SE XXIII, 148; *Civilization and Its Discontents,* SE XXI, 118–119.
2. *Civilization and Its Discontents,* SE XXI, 135.
3. *Three Essays on the Theory of Sexuality,* SE VII, 191.
4. *An Outline of Psycho-Analysis,* SE XXIII, 152; *Introductory Lectures on Psycho-Analysis,* SE XVI, 320–321.
5. *Three Essays,* SE VII, 163ff., 233; see also *Sexuality in the Aetiology of Neuroses,* SE III, 268.
6. *Three Essays,* SE VII, 167–168, 232–233.
7. *Civilization and Its Discontents,* SE XXI, 99.
8. *Group Psychology and the Analysis of the Ego,* SE XVIII, 121.
9. *Id.* at 92.
10. *The Republic,* tr. F. Cornford (London: Oxford University Press, 1974), book V, 463.
11. *The Politics of Aristotle,* tr. E. Barker (London: Oxford University Press, 1974), book II, iii, sec. 4.
12. *The Philosophy of David Hume,* ed. V. Chappell (New York: Modern Library, 1963), 264.
13. Karl Popper, *The Open Society and Its Enemies* (Princeton: Princeton University Press, 1966), vol. 2, 235.
14. Hannah Arendt, *The Human Condition* (Chicago: University of Chicago Press, 1958), 51–52.
15. *Ibid.*
16. Rieff, *Freud: The Mind of the Moralist,* 234.
17. *Civilization and Its Discontents,* SE XXI, 110.
18. *Three Essays,* SE VII, Preface to the Fourth Edition, 134.
19. I owe the formulation of this point to Draenos, 121.
20. *Civilization and Its Discontents,* SE XXI, 145.
21. *Ibid.*

CHAPTER TWO: *Eros and the Psychology of Love*

1. *Group Psychology,* SE XVIII, 106.
2. *On Narcissism,* SE XIV, 87.
3. *On the Universal Tendency to Debasement in the Sphere of Love,* SE XI, 180.

4. *The Ego and the Id*, SE XIX, 31.

5. *Group Psychology*, SE XVIII, 105.

6. *Civilization and Its Discontents*, SE XXI, 66–67.

7. *Three Essays*, SE VII, 222.

8. *On Narcissism*, SE XIV, 90.

9. *Id.* at 88.

10. *Group Psychology*, SE XVIII, 111–116.

11. *The Tendency to Debasement in Love*, SE XI, 183.

12. *Id.* at 184.

13. *A Special Type of Choice of Object Made by Men*, SE XI, 166.

14. *The Tendency to Debasement in Love*, SE XI, 180. The significance of this paper first came to my attention through a reading of Rieff's *Freud: The Mind of the Moralist*. The analysis in my text first tracks that given by Rieff, 158ff., then partially dissents from that analysis. The debt I owe to Rieff's work in particular will be evident to any reader of this work familiar with his writings.

15. *The Tendency to Debasement in Love*, SE XI, 180.

16. *Id.* at 181.

17. *Ibid.*

18. *Ibid;* see also *Civilized Sexual Morality and Modern Nervousness*, CP II, 87.

19. The distinction between triggering and predisposing causes in Freud's theory of neurosis is brought out clearly and succinctly in Richard Wollheim, *Sigmund Freud* (New York: The Viking Press, 1971), 151–158; see also *The Schreber Case*, SE XII, 67.

20. *The Tendency to Debasement in Love*, SE XI, 181–182.

21. *Ibid.*

22. Rieff, *Freud: The Mind of the Moralist*, 158–168.

23. *Id.* at 159–160.

24. *Ibid.*

25. *Id.* at 160, 166.

26. *Id.* at 159.

27. *Id.* at 160.

28. *Id.* at 223.

29. *Group Psychology*, SE XVIII, 105.

30. *Instincts and Their Vicissitudes*, SE XIV, 134; *On Narcissism*, SE XIV, 100.

31. *Instincts and Their Vicissitudes*, SE XIV, 136.

32. *Id.* at 139.

33. *Group Psychology*, SE XVIII, 105.

34. *Instincts and Their Vicissitudes*, SE XIV, 138–139.

35. *The Economic Problem in Masochism*, CP II, 256.

36. *Female Sexuality*, CP V, 254.

37. Brown, *Life Against Death*, 53. Although I disagree with Brown on this notion of preambivalence, his is the only account I know that highlights the Freudian concept of identification and its significance as a desire to be at one with another person. Unfortunately, Brown takes the desire for oneness to its nihilistic conclusion and would appear to follow Spinoza in seeking to achieve a final state of satisfaction that would end the self to be satisfied. This book attempts to follow much of the Brown reading of Freud, stripped of Brown's own eschatological bent.

38. *The Ego and the Id*, SE XIX, 29.

39. *Group Psychology*, SE XVIII, 105.

40. *Instincts and Their Vicissitudes*, SE XIV, 138.

41. *Group Psychology*, SE XVIII, 105.

42. *Civilization and Its Discontents*, SE XXI, 68.

43. *Ibid.*

44. *On Narcissism*, SE XIV, 100.

45. I owe this point to J. Laplanche and J. B. Pontalis, *The Language of Psychoanalysis*, tr. D. Smith (New York: W. W. Norton & Co., Inc., 1973), 255.

46. *On Narcissism*, SE XIV, 100.

47. Rieff, *Freud: The Mind of the Moralist*, 158.

48. *Mourning and Melancholia*, CP IV, 166.

49. *Id.* at 154.

50. Ricoeur, *Freud and Philosophy*, 132.

51. *On Narcissism*, SE XIV, 76–77.

52. *The Ego and the Id*, SE XIX, 31.

53. *Id.* at 30 n. 1; 46–47.

54. Laplanche and Pontalis, 338; see also *Group Psychology*, SE XVIII, 130–131.

55. Laplanche and Pontalis, 255, 338.

56. *On Narcissism*, SE XIV, 76–77.

CHAPTER THREE: *Death and the Psychology of Cruelty*

1. *Analysis of a Phobia in a Five-Year-Old Boy*, SE X, 113.

2. *Civilization and Its Discontents*, SE XXI, 122.

3. *Id.* at 134.

4. *Id.* at 118.

5. *Id.* at 119–120, 122.

6. *Id.* at 119–120; *Three Essays*, SE VII, 157–160; 192–193.

7. *Three Essays*, SE VII, 159.

8. *Civilization and Its Discontents*, SE XXI, 113. Freud goes on to note one possible exception to the aggressive basis of all love relations: "the mother's relation to the male child." But this remark is left unexplained.

9. *Economic Problem in Masochism*, CP II, 260.

10. *Ibid.*

11. *Civilization and Its Discontents*, SE XXI, 119.

12. *Id.* at 121.

13. *Economic Problem in Masochism*, CP II, 260.

14. *New Introductory Lectures on Psycho-Analysis*, SE XXII, 105.

15. *Civilization and Its Discontents*, SE XXI, 103.

16. *Id.* at 141.

17. *Id.* at 109.

18. *Id.* at 111.

19. *Id.* at 112.

20. *Id.* at 112.

21. *Female Sexuality*, CP V, 256.

22. *Group Psychology*, SE XVIII, 105.

23. *Civilization and Its Discontents*, SE XXI, 124.

24. *The Ego and the Id*, SE XIX, 54.

25. See, e.g., *Introductory Lectures*, SE XVI, 354.

26. *New Introductory Lectures*, SE XXII, 62.

27. *Civilization and Its Discontents*, SE XXI, 130.

28. *Id.* at 129.

29. *Id.* at 129–130.

30. *Id.* at 138.

31. *Id.* at 136.

32. *Id.* at 123.

33. *The Ego and the Id*, SE XIX, 54.

34. *Economic Problem in Masochism*, CP II, 267.

35. *Ibid.*

36. *The Ego and the Id*, SE XIX, 53.

37. Ricoeur, *Freud and Philosophy*, 299.

38. *Civilization and Its Discontents*, SE XXI, 127–128.

39. *The Passing of the Oedipus-Complex*, CP II, 274.

40. *Id.* at 275.

41. *New Introductory Lectures*, SE XXII, 129.

42. Dorothy Dinnerstein, *The Mermaid and the Minotaur: Sexual Arrangements and Human Malaise* (New York: Harper & Row, 1976), p. 41.

43. *Analysis of a Phobia in a Five-Year-Old Boy*, SE X, 126.

44. *Id.* at 10.

45. *Introductory Lectures*, SE XVI, 337.

46. *Notes upon a Case of Obsessional Neurosis*, CP III, 293.

47. *Id.* at 318.

48. *New Introductory Lectures*, SE XXII, 61.

49. *Dostoevsky and Parricide*, SE XXI, 177.

50. *Id.* at 187, n. 2.

51. *Id.* at 185.

52. This section elaborates on Alasdair MacIntyre's work on both Nietzsche's and Freud's significance for moral theory. See MacIntyre, *After Virtue* (Notre Dame: Notre Dame University Press, 1981), 107, and his "Freud," *Encyclopedia of Philosophy*, vol. 3-4, 252.

53. *The Letters of Sigmund Freud and Arnold Zweig*, tr. Professor and Mrs. W. D. Robson-Scott (London: The Hogarth Press and the Institute of Psycho-Analysis, 1970), 23.

54. *Introductory Lectures*, SE XVI, 434.

55. *Economic Problem in Masochism*, CP II, 264.

56. Kant, *Groundwork of the Metaphysic of Morals*, tr. H. J. Paton (New York: Harper & Row, 1964), 92–98. For a lucid account of Kant's moral philosophy as it relates to human freedom, see Michael Sandel, *Liberalism and the Limits of Justice* (London: Cambridge University Press, 1982), 2–11.

57. quoted in Sandel, 6.

58. Kant, 63.

59. MacIntyre, "Freud," *Encyclopedia of Philosophy*, vol. 3-4, 252.

60. *Civilization and Its Discontents*, SE XXI, 144.

CHAPTER FOUR: *Eros, Death, and Politics*

1. *Civilization and Its Discontents*, SE XXI, 108.

2. *Id.* at 108–109.

3. *Group Psychology*, SE XVIII, 121.

4. *Civilization and Its Discontents*, SE XXI, 109–110.

5. *Id.* at 145.

6. Geza Roheim, *The Origin and Function of Culture* (New York: Doubleday and Co., 1971), 109.

7. *Moses and Monotheism*, SE XXIII, 98.

8. *Group Psychology*, SE XVIII, 121.
9. *Civilization and Its Discontents*, SE XXI, 99.
10. *Moses and Monotheism*, SE XXIII, 131.
11. *Totem and Taboo*, SE XIII, 141–142.
12. *Moses and Monotheism*, SE XXIII, 82.
13. Marcuse, *Eros and Civilization*, 61.
14. *Moses and Monotheism*, SE XXIII, 99–101, 132.
15. *Id.* at 99–100.
16. *Id.* at 84; *Totem and Taboo*, SE XIII, 161.
17. *Moses and Monotheism*, SE XXIII, 101.
18. Marcuse, 54, 120.
19. *Civilization and Its Discontents*, SE XXI, 145.
20. *Group Psychology*, SE XVIII, 76.
21. *Id.* at 117.
22. *Ibid.*
23. *Id.* at 91–92.
24. *Civilization and Its Discontents*, SE XXI, 116.
25. *Ibid.*
26. *Group Psychology*, SE XVIII, 100.
27. *Id.* at 116.
28. *Id.* at 123.
29. *Id.* at 88.
30. *Thoughts for the Times on War and Death*, CP IV, 294, 300.
31. *Id.* at 299–300.
32. *Id.* at 289.
33. Ernest Jones, *The Life and Work of Sigmund Freud* (New York: Basic Books, Inc., 1955), vol. 2, 170–171.
34. *Thoughts on War and Death*, CP IV, 293.
35. *Id.* at 292–293.
36. *Id.* at 293–294.
37. Jones, 171.
38. *Thoughts on War and Death*, CP IV, 306.
39. *Id.* at 307.
40. *Id.* at 292.
41. *Ibid.*
42. *Civilization and Its Discontents*, SE XXI, 114.
43. *Id.* at 115.

CHAPTER FIVE: *Psychoanalysis and Religion*

1. *Civilization and Its Discontents,* SE XXI, 75, 76.
2. *One of the Difficulties of Psycho-Analysis,* CP IV, 350–352.
3. *Id.* at 355.
4. *The Future of an Illusion,* SE XXI, 24.
5. *Id.* at 30.
6. *Totem and Taboo,* SE XIII, 132.
7. *Ibid.*
8. *Moses and Monotheism,* SE XXIII, 133.
9. *Id.* at 88–89.
10. *Id.* at 113.
11. *Id.* at 134–135.
12. *Id.* at 58.
13. *Id.* at 101.
14. *Ibid.*
15. *Id.* at 86.
16. *Totem and Taboo,* SE XIII, 161.
17. *Id.* at 160.
18. Laplanche and Pontalis, *The Language of Psychoanalysis,* 315.
19. *Totem and Taboo,* SE XIII, 160.
20. *The Future of an Illusion,* SE XXI, 44.
21. *Id.* at 43.
22. *Id.* at 49.
23. *Id.* at 54.
24. *Leonardo da Vinci and a Memory of His Childhood,* SE XI, 124–125.
25. *The Future of an Illusion,* SE XXI, 38–39.
26. *Id.* at 39.
27. *Ibid.*
28. *Id.* at 44.
29. *Civilization and Its Discontents,* SE XXI, 74.
30. *Ibid.*
31. *Id.* at 64.
32. *Id.* at 65.
33. *Id.* at 68.
34. *Id.* at 72.
35. *Totem and Taboo,* SE XIII, xv.

CHAPTER SIX: *Sublimation: A Way Out?*

1. *On Narcissism,* SE XIV, 95.
2. Ricoeur, *Freud and Philosophy,* 483–484.
3. Daniel Yankelovich and William Barrett, *Ego and Instinct: The Psychoanalytic View of Human Nature—Revised* (New York: Random House, 1970), 312.
4. As Peter Madison has shown (*Freud's Concept of Repression and Defense,* Minneapolis: University of Minnesota Press, 1961), the difference between repression and other "defense mechanisms" (conversion, reaction formation, projection, and isolation) is not always clear in Freud. In the early *Studies on Hysteria,* written with Breuer, repression referred only to the particular mechanism of hysterical amnesia, only to unconsciously motivated forgetting. But the 1915 paper *Repression* made repression almost synonymous with defense against the instincts in general, treating conversion and the other mechanisms as "forms of repression." Not until the addendum to *Inhibitions, Symptoms and Anxiety* (1926) does Freud revive the term "defense," once again restricting repression to hysterical amnesia. However, as Madison has shown, the *text* of this 1926 work itself continues to refer to the other defense mechanisms as examples of repression.

    For purposes of clarity, I follow Madison's suggestion and see Freud as separating out repressive defenses (amnesia, conversion, and the others listed above) from allegedly nonrepressive defenses such as sublimation or rational condemnation. The hallmark of repressive defenses is their use of *omissions from or distortions in consciousness as a means of ego protection.* From this point of view, sublimation's promised "way out" is a way into consciousness.

5. *Inhibitions, Symptoms and Anxiety,* SE XX, 91.
6. *Repression,* CP IV, 90.
7. *Three Essays,* SE VII, 178.
8. *Id.* at 238.
9. *Id.* at 178.
10. Yankelovich and Barrett, 312.
11. *Civilizations and Its Discontents,* SE XXI, 144.
12. *The Ego and the Id,* SE XIX, 30.
13. *Id.* at 46, 54–55.
14. Yankelovich and Barrett, 313.
15. *Ibid.*
16. It is illuminating in hindsight that the early Freud was not a stranger to chemical treatments. Upon his return from Paris to Vienna in 1886, he set

about treating his "nervous patients" with electrotherapy, baths, and massages. Jones, *The Life and Work of Sigmund Freud,* vol. 1, 235.

17. *Beyond the Pleasure Principle,* SE XVIII, 14–15.

18. *Id.* at 16.

19. *Id.* at 15.

20. *Leonardo da Vinci,* SE XI, 74–75.

21. Quoted in *id.* at 69.

22. *Id.* at 75.

23. *Id.* at 74.

24. *Id.* at 75.

25. *Id.* at 76.

26. Ricoeur, 336–337.

27. *Leonardo da Vinci,* SE XI, 131.

28. In comparing the work that goes into dreams with the technique of jokes, Freud writes, "The dream is a completely asocial psychical product. Wit, on the other hand, is the most social of all pleasure-seeking psychic functions. . . . It must therefore bind itself to the condition of intelligibility." Brown, *Life Against Death,* 61.

29. *Leonardo da Vinci,* SE XI, 110.

30. *Id.* at 117, 111.

31. *Id.* at 117–118.

32. Ricoeur, 174.

33. *Introductory Lectures,* SE XVI, 376.

34. quoted in Brown, *Life Against Death, p. 62.*

35. *See* Lionel Trilling, *The Liberal Imagination* (New York: The Viking Press, 1950), 34.

36. *Three Essays,* SE VII, 134.

37. "The Symposium," in B. Jowett, tr., *The Dialogues of Plato* (New York: Random House, 1937), p. 335.

38. Anders Nygren, *Agape and Eros* (Philadelphia: Westminster Press, 1953), 77.

39. "The Symposium," in Jowett, 329.

40. *Ibid.*

41. *On Narcissism,* SE XIV, 95.

42. *Civilization and Its Discontents,* SE XXI, 97.

43. *Id.* at 79–80.

44. Marcuse, *Eros and Civilization,* 190.

45. *Civilization and Its Discontents,* SE XXI, 80 n. 1.

46. Marcuse, 190.
47. *Id.* at 196.

CHAPTER SEVEN: *Therapy and Freedom*

1. *Five Lectures on Psycho-Analysis,* SE XI, 48.
2. *Introductory Lectures,* SE XVI, 432–433.
3. *Id.* at 455.
4. *The Justification for Detaching from Neurasthenia a Particular Syndrome: The Anxiety-Neurosis,* CP I, 98.
5. *Id.* at 97–98.
6. *Civilized Sexual Morality,* CP II, 87; *Sexuality in the Aetiology of Neuroses,* SE III, 277.
7. *Studies on Hysteria,* SE II, 8, 201–202.
8. *Id.* at 35, 37, 40.
9. *A Case of Successful Treatment by Hypnotism,* CP V, 33ff.
10. *Introductory Lectures,* SE XVI, 365.
11. *Repression,* SE XIV, 149–150; *On the History of the Psycho-Analytic Movement,* SE XIV, 16; *An Outline of Psycho-Analysis,* SE XXIII, 174.
12. *The Defence Neuro-Psychoses,* CP I, 62.
13. *Id.* at 66; *Fragment of an Analysis of a Case of Hysteria,* SE VII, 115.
14. *Id.* at 115.
15. *Introductory Lectures,* SE XVI, 261–264.
16. *Further Remarks on the Defence Neuro-Psychoses,* CP I, 157.
17. *See* Jeffrey M. Masson, *The Assault on Truth: Freud's Suppression of the Seduction Theory* (New York: Farrar, Straus, Giroux, 1984), 134. For cases where Freud accepts reports of sexual advances against children, *see Studies on Hysteria,* SE II, 134 n. 2; *Fragment of an Analysis of Hysteria,* SE VII, 25–26, 28; *From the History of an Infantile Neurosis,* SE XVII, 21 ("[H]is seduction by his sister was certainly not a phantasy."). For Freud's rejection of an adult's side of the story, see SE VII, 25–26, 28.
18. *An Outline of Psycho-Analysis,* SE XXIII, 152.
19. *Three Essays,* SE VII, 225.
20. *Id.* at 171; *Types of Neurotic Nosogenesis,* CP II, 120.
21. *Fragment of an Analysis of a Case of Hysteria,* SE VII, 28.
22. *Id.* at 35, 57.
23. *An Outline of Psycho-Analysis,* SE XXIII, 174.
24. *Introductory Lectures,* SE XVI, p. 450.
25. *Ibid.*

26. *The Question of Lay Analysis*, SE XX, p. 226.

27. *Introductory Lectures*, SE XVI, p. 454.

28. *Ibid.*

29. *Notes upon a Case of Obsessional Neurosis*, SE X, 209.

30. *A Case of Successful Treatment by Hypnotism*, CP V, 33ff.

31. *Introductory Lectures*, SE XVI, 451.

32. *Id.* at 453.

33. *An Outline of Psycho-Analysis*, SE XXIII, 174.

34. *Ibid.*

35. *The Psychopathology of Everyday Life*, SE VI, 254.

36. *Introductory Lectures*, SE XV, 28.

37. *Id.* at 49.

38. Habermas, *Knowledge and Human Interests*, Chapter 11 generally, 246–274. I have relied heavily on Habermas' argument for my remarks in this section on Freud and causal explanations.

39. *The Psychopathology of Everyday Life*, SE VI, 219.

40. *Id.* at 250–251.

41. Habermas, 271.

42. Shklar, *Freedom and Independence: A Study of the Political Ideas of Hegel's "Phenomenology of Mind,"* (Cambridge: Cambridge University Press, 1976), 9–10.

43. Ricoeur, *Freud and Philosophy*, 459–468.

44. *Recommendations for Physicians on the Psycho-Analytic Method of Treatment*, CP II, 331.

45. Quoted in Paul Roazen, *Freud: Political and Social Thought* (New York: Vintage Books, 1968), 292.

46. *Introductory Lectures*, SE XVI, 434.

47. Ricoeur, 280.

48. *Inhibitions, Symptoms and Anxiety*, SE XX, 95.

49. *New Introductory Lectures*, SE XXII, 171.

50. *The Question of Lay Analysis*, SE XX, 201.

51. *Studies on Hysteria*, SE II, 305.

CHAPTER EIGHT: *Eros, Friendship, and Citizenship*

1. *Civilization and Its Discontents*, SE XXI, 144.

2. *Ibid.*

3. *Ibid.*

4. *Id.* at 103.

5. *Id.* at 109.

6. *Id.* at 109–110.

7. *The Nichomachean Ethics,* tr. Ross (London: Oxford University Press, 1925), 193 (viii, sec. 1).

8. Because of his views on the inequality of men and women, Aristotle could allow husband and wife to be friends only of the imperfect sort. As opposed to the modern view, Aristotle therefore made friendship a more complete, because more equal, intimacy than marriage. I owe this observation to my colleague, Susan Moller Okin.

9. *Id.* at 200 (viii, sec. 5).

10. *Ibid.*

11. *Ibid.*

12. *Id.* at 207 (viii, sec. 9).

13. *Id.* at 243 (ix, sec. 10).

14. *Id.* at 243 (ix, sec. 10).

15. Sandel, *Liberalism and the Limits of Justice,* 183.

16. I owe this point to MacIntyre, *After Virtue,* pp. 146–147.

CONCLUSION: *The Limits of Liberation*

1. Thomas Hobbes, *Leviathan* (London: Collier-Macmillan, 1962), 159.

2. *Wilhelm Reich, The Function of the Orgasm,* tr. V. Carfagno (New York: Simon & Schuster, 1975), 196.

Index

132 - 1950's conformity